CO-HABITATS

Edited by
Hashim Sarkis and
Ala Tannir

HOW WE DO

LIVE TOGETHER IN...

ADDIS ABABA

AL AZRAQ CAMP

BEIRUT

HONG KONG

INDIA

MEXICO/EGYPT/NIGERIA

NEW YORK

PRISHTINA

RIO DE JANEIRO

SÃO PAULO

VENICE

La Biennale di Venezia

PRESIDENT
Roberto Cicutto

BOARD
Luigi Brugnaro
Vice President

Claudia Ferrazzi
Luca Zaia

AUDITORS' COMMITTEE
Jair Lorenco
President

Stefania Bortoletti
Anna Maria Como

DIRECTOR GENERAL
Andrea Del Mercato

**ARTISTIC DIRECTOR
OF THE
ARCHITECTURE DEPARTMENT**
Hashim Sarkis

CONTENTS

Co-Habitats

Hashim Sarkis

Co-

This book is based on a simple premise. The architecture around us contains an abundance of answers to the question, *"How will we live together?"* We just need to look. We have been creating, inhabiting, and readjusting these spaces over centuries. It is important to examine where and how we have succeeded and where and how we have failed.

The book documents research at several universities, institutions, and beyond by professors, students, and individuals who have been looking closely at locations they have been studying and inhabiting for a long time. They identify buildings, public spaces, networks, spatial habits, monuments, and homesteads that represent our inherent capabilities as architects and citizens alike to shape spaces for cohabitation.

The settlements studied here are different in size. They range from discreet open spaces, to refugee settlements, to whole cities, to cross continental regions. The range in scale goes beyond the subject to include the scales of cohabitation. Inside the smallest of urban spaces one can find a way of connecting to the entire world. These studies also suggest that architecture is capable of operating at different scales simultaneously. One can be at once in a house and watching a World Cup soccer game while looking over the community garden of the cooperative building. Inside the tiniest kitchen of a house in a squatter settlement in Lagos, the arrangement on the table can transport one to another part of the world.

The essays therefore document contexts, places in which we spend a lot of time and which we come to recognize and appreciate directly and inadvertently, but they also highlight the transcendental qualities of these spaces, their ability to project out of context, and to propose alternative realities to the one we inhabit.

Whether as protesters creatively appropriating and reshaping urban spaces, as commuters from different ethnic communities encountering each other on their way to work and weaving connections under a sequestered city, or as refugees from various locations redefining a collective home out of borrowed architectures, this book celebrates the human ingenuity of inhabiting place by constantly reinventing it.

Habitats 7

However, this book also laments the fact that we are being increasingly challenged in our abilities to build such spaces of the collective imaginary. The authors of these essays look for them hard and deep in the interstices of cities and also describe the regrettable impact of their erosion on the citizens and the struggles to recreate them in an increasingly privatized public realm.

In his seminal book *The Tyranny of Merit,* philosopher Michael J. Sandel shares the same dismay. He argues that "public spaces that gather people together across class, race, ethnicity, and faith are few and far between. Four decades of market driven globalization has brought inequalities of income and wealth so pronounced that they lead us into separate ways of life. Those who are affluent and those of modest means rarely encounter one another in the course of the day. We live and work and shop and play in different places; our children go to different schools. And when the meritocratic sorting machine has done its work, those on top find it hard to resist the thought that they deserve their place as well. This feeds a politics so poisonous and a partisanship so intense that many now regard marriages across party lines as more troubling than marrying outside the faith. It is little wonder we have lost the ability to reason together about large public questions, or even to listen to one another."[1]

The political philosopher's version of this lamentation ascertains an almost causal connection between the disintegration of common space and the fragmentation of the common good. It underlines our responsibilities as architects to multiply the possibilities of interaction and encounter across differences and borders. In that sense the authors of this book lay out a repertoire of possibilities, a richly architectural one, to reclaim the common good by exposing, through their analytic creativity, how we have been doing it all along.

1   Michael J. Sandel, *The Tyranny of Merit: What's Become of the Common Good?* (New York: Farrar, Straus and Giroux, 2020), 226.

Hashim Sarkis

Co-

Habitats

9

ADDIS ABABA

Quo Addis? Conflicts of Coexistence

Marc Angélil
and Cary Siress

Addis

For a brief moment, all eyes were on Addis, for better or worse. Whereas the 2019 Nobel Peace Prize had just been awarded to Ethiopian Prime Minister Abiy Ahmed for having resolved long-standing border tensions with neighboring Eritrea, Ethiopia was still being torn apart by mounting ethnic violence within its own borders. And while the spotlight was on a young politician claiming to be a leader capable of unifying a divided land and ushering in a new era of empowerment for a people long repressed, age-old tribal rivalries had flared up once again, leading not only to widespread bloodshed in the capital, but also threatening to displace vast portions of the population throughout the country. At the center of the conflict was the question of political, religious, and ethnic identity. Ethno-nationalist movements fighting for their local autonomy fiercely contested Abiy's campaign for a unified national party, resulting in an identity-based standoff of one versus many.

Such ambivalences notwithstanding, the fanfare surrounding the Peace Prize and the flurry of media coverage of the revolts seemed to have missed the more fundamental issue of Ethiopia's precarious standing in the world altogether—a not so insignificant blind spot shrouding the chronic dependence on foreign powers that has plagued the country for more than a century. Ethiopia, as a matter of fact, has repeatedly been a site of exploitation by outside actors. It has undergone a rapid succession of regime changes and been exposed to competing politico-economic models that came with transitions of power, which in sum have turned the land into a veritable experiment in nation-building that still confounds the very question of identity today.

There are many iterations of Ethiopia, and they have come in hybrid forms under imperialism, colonialism, socialism, and capitalism. Each iteration engendered an attendant imaginary concerning what a nation should be in political, economic, and spatial terms, along with a governing disposition premised above all on its marked distinction from

following: Merkato in Addis Ababa, one of Africa's largest open markets, was originally established to house indigenous populations during the Italian occupation in the late 1930s; considered valuable real estate, the neighborhood is currently being transformed into a high-end commercial district, with small-scale vendors having managed, at least for the time being, to retain a foothold in the market.

Ababa

Marc Angélil and Cary Siress

Addis

Ababa

the previous mindset. During the rapid succession of transitions, it is as if the country underwent its own series of *mirror stages* in which identities were imposed, discovered, appropriated, erased, and reinvented. Across its history of transformative shifts, the country entered into relations with various foreign actors, either by choice or by force, giving rise to different forms of dependency and engendering a legacy of reliance that continues to this day via programs of relief aid, technical assistance, legal guidance, development loans, foreign direct investment, infrastructure financing, and planning expertise.

Having become a nexus for competing interests, and with new scrambles for Africa well underway, telltale tensions have arisen concerning which direction the nation might take to resolve its many dilemmas. Ethiopia still finds itself torn between the desire for autonomy and the reality of dependence, between the desire for maintaining cultural identity and the reality of being ever tempted by mainstream values, between the desire for resistance and the tendency toward compliance with directives from abroad.

Such tensions are nowhere more evident than in Addis Ababa, which is de facto a palimpsest of identities past and present, a rich hybrid of fragments posited as so many expressions of power. The aggregated traces of interventions by former and current regimes have made the city a physical amalgam born of competing ideologies, each in its own way aiming to establish a distinct political authority and territorial identity. In this sense, looking into the mirror of Ethiopia— and specifically, that of Addis Ababa—yields a blurred image at best, a hazy composite of forces and counterforces that have put the nation in its present-day quandary and produced so many of the internal tensions both social and physical that remain unresolved.

However Prime Minister Abiy ultimately responds to current tensions, he will inevitably have to build on the wild hybrid that Addis Ababa has become as the face of a fractured nation. He will have to confront the tangle of aggregates that each successive regime has left behind, and this while trying to craft a new identity for the nation. In his effort to establish new

ties with foreign partners, he will also have to take stock of how grand visions of the past have enmeshed the country in a web of dependencies that in effect have robbed Ethiopia of its own identity. The prime minister might reflect, for example, on the "grand projects" of one of his recent predecessors, Meles Zenawi, which were celebrated on a large banner at Zenawi's state funeral in 2012 as a veritable collection of architectural and infrastructural trophies.

As if paying tribute to a deceased emperor, the event raised national mourning to the status of pageantry to honor the late architect of Ethiopian development. Curiously enough, the commemorative banner was hung in the same place as an earlier one depicting Marx, Engels, and Lenin that had been mounted by the communist regime in the 1970s in what was then Revolution Square. Zenawi's banner, in essence, replaced these three figures of socialist thought with capitalist icons of his modernization program. Suspended above a crowd of dignitaries, including African leaders and military troops parading before the coffin, Zenawi's banner portrayed the prime minister amid large-scale projects initiated during his time in office.

following: Banner at Meskel Square (formerly Revolution Square) during Meles Zenawi's state funeral, with the former prime minister shown among notable development projects undertaken during his term in office; the translation of the inscription in Amharic reads, "What you envisioned is vivid and immediate; we will realize it with perseverance," September 3, 2012.

Shown on the far left was the 2012 addition to the African Union headquarters, a high-profile gift from the People's Republic of China offered in gratitude for Africa's support of China's entry into the United Nations some decades ago. The former assembly hall of the Organization of African Unity (OAU) had been designed by Italian architect Arturo Mezzedimi as a symbol of modern Ethiopia under the reign of Emperor Haile Selassie in the early 1960s. Haile Selassie had returned to Ethiopia from exile during the Italian occupation (1936–1941) and founded the OAU, whose mission, considering the continent's history of colonization, was meant to secure the sovereignty of African states. One wonders today, if such "gifts" from China do not presage yet another round of modern-day subjugation by new means.

Ababa

የጀመርከው ትልም ብሩሀና ቅር

Marc Angélil and Cary Siress

Addis

Ababa

Apartment blocks of the Addis Ababa Grand Housing Program, launched in 2004, featured in the center of the memorial banner. Among other partners including the World Bank and UN-Habitat, this project was primarily supported by the German Technical Cooperation Agency, which provided technical and financial assistance in accordance with conventional North-South aid policies. In this case, German engineers, architects, and managers were called in to prepare manuals, construction documents, schedules, budgets, and material specifications, all being the preferred channels for transferring norms from developed to developing world regions. Construction materials and building products were imported as well in compliance with international standards, perhaps explaining why thousands of Chinese-made toilet bowls were shipped in for installation in housing project after housing project.

The Grand Ethiopian Renaissance Dam—under construction since 2011—appeared on the far right of the banner as a cornerstone of Ethiopia's future electricity infrastructure. Financed via government bonds issued to local and foreign investors, the dam's construction was initially awarded to an Italian company, without competitive bidding. Due to the project's geopolitical ramifications, particularly in view of its potentially detrimental impact on downstream countries along the Nile, the Ethiopian government was unable to secure funding from the usual international financial institutions (USAID, World Bank, IMF). Therefore, when faced with budget shortfalls, Ethiopia turned to China for loans made available through the Asia Infrastructure Investment Bank to finance the dam's hydro-mechanical equipment—to be realized by a French company—and, most importantly, the nationwide energy distribution network. Concerning the latter, the concessional loans were made in accordance with what is known as the "Angola Mode"—an arrangement stipulating that Chinese credit be issued only when used for projects realized with Chinese construction companies, and a scheme guaranteeing that outgoing money returns to China, albeit with interest.

Marc Angélil and Cary Siress

While all the projects are shown draped with the flowing ribbon of the Ethiopian flag to underline the nation's avowed sovereignty, each depended to a great extent on funds and technical assistance from abroad. What is less apparent in this *mise-en-scène* is the totalizing operation driving it, which is predicated on integrating those "stranded" regions of the world into the global market. This operation, according to which everything must be cast within the force field of capitalism, is a function of the empire-building machinery of our time. So, the reimaging of Ethiopia, along with the imposing political order that former Prime Minister Zenawi eventually established, was but one episode, and a bitter one at that, of a geopolitical macrophysics at work wherever it was deemed lucrative. One finds its deposits embroidered into management protocols, policy legislation, financial instruments, contract stipulations, and technical manuals, all of which steer countries like Ethiopia along their particular development path. In the case of Ethiopia, these techniques have set the terms for the nation's perpetual "remaking" and still comprise the medium for its control as a "project," whereby alliance-building and development cooperation, as necessary as they may be, most often engender what could be called a *dependency syndrome*.

Current Prime Minister Abiy and his opponents alike could learn much from this lesson. Yet, the ongoing concern about how to live together in a region marred by provincial infighting over one identity or many identities misses the larger issue of systemic exploitation of all parties. That said, Abiy is now taking the more tried (and troubling) route of his predecessors in deploying capital-led development to upgrade the capital city, albeit in a piecemeal manner, via targeted, high-profile projects. A few months after his election in 2018, the new prime minister announced his vision to beautify or give a facelift to Addis Ababa to make the city literally more attractive for foreign investment. His first symbolic gesture was to upgrade the historic palace of Emperor Menelik II under the catchphrases "greening" and "refurbishment," an act of branding

following: Supporters of the Ethiopian Workers' Party in front of large portraits of Marx, Engels, and Lenin in Revolution Square in 1987, which would later be named Meskel Square after the fall of the socialist regime, Addis Ababa, 1987.

Ababa

19

20   *Marc Angélil and Cary Siress*   Addis

Ababa

Marc Angélil and Cary Siress Addis

that plays on Addis Ababa's namesake "The New Flower" to recast the imperial grounds and eventually the whole city itself as a lush tourist attraction.

In a similar vein, Abiy moved swiftly to court investors from the United Arab Emirates to upgrade the site of the former train station—another structure built in the early twentieth century during the reign of Menelik II—and turn it into the crown jewel of the La Gare megadevelopment entertainment, business, and high-rise housing district. All of this will be made possible by more blank-slate development meant to rid the city of unwanted people and places, such as the drab Soviet-style housing blocks from the 1970s and their low-income populations, official claims to the contrary notwithstanding. Interestingly, this project was celebrated on China Global Television Network (CGTN) to highlight the advent of a new business culture in Ethiopia, one driven by joint ventures with outside partners that currently keep the host country in the position of minority stakeholder.

This imbalance aside, Abiy's makeover strategy appears to be paying off for the moment, inasmuch as the People's Republic of China has also moved in to capitalize on his beautification campaign after winning the bid to develop select stretches of Addis Ababa's main river. Announced in October 2019, the Riverside project—though initially awarded to an Italian company—will be realized by China Communications Construction Company and made possible with grants as well as loans from the Chinese government. It goes without saying that this venture will bring with it the demolition of low-rise settlements in the area and enforced displacement of their poor resident populations. In so doing, the project will essentially gentrify the river basin, which is conceived as the infrastructural spine of a new, high-end real estate corridor; it will be outfitted with bicycle paths and walkways that will wind through the capital past all those opulent properties still in the planning phase.

top: Italian architect Arturo Mezzedimi presenting a model of the Organization of African Unity *in Addis Ababa to Secretary-General U Thant, February, 1969.*

bottom: China Global Television Network (CGTN) reporting on the La Gare *luxury development complex to be built on the former site of the Addis Ababa train station by Eagle Hills, a real estate investment and development company based in Abu Dhabi, November 23, 2018.*

Ababa

So goes the new wave of urbanization in Addis Ababa. And Abiy seems to be resolute about continuing along this particular path of development. Then again, the new prime minister did not win the Nobel Peace Prize for nothing. Not only did he successfully broker a peace deal with Eritrea, he also introduced key reforms at home in a very short time: he revoked longstanding repressive laws, bridged communal and sectarian divides, promoted democratic processes at all levels of society, invited alienated ethnic groups back to the negotiating table, freed imprisoned political dissidents, and appointed a significant number of women to high administrative posts. Such measures are clearly meant to distinguish his administration from those of his predecessors. Moreover, they have given Ethiopians real hope for a better life and a measurable change in fortune for all of Ethiopia, if not for Africa as a whole.

For this to become a reality, however, and for Africa to really be "rising," other more equitable modes of cooperation among all stakeholders within the global community must be devised so that Africa might overcome its dependency syndrome—let alone the never-ending debt entrapment, ever-widening disparities between rich and poor, and endlessly-proliferating environmental degradation. When tasked with the challenge of aligning democratic reforms with the imperatives of a prevalent model of economic growth now global in scale, it is undoubtedly easy to conflate the "free" of the "free market" with genuine freedoms, thus making it hard to say no to the highest bidder.

The prevailing imaginary of "developmentalism" banks on this very conflation to keep uneven relationships in place between dominant and dominated partners. Moreover, the prevailing mode of development is about containing and controlling unruly realities of places like Addis Ababa through

PROJECT CREDITS

Marc Angélil, Katharina Blümke, Dirk Hebel, Felix Heisel, Jenny Rodenhouse, and Bisrat Kifle Woldeyessus, with Willy Abraham, Nikolai Babunovic, Emmanuel Bekele Fulea, Uta Bogenrieder, Sascha Delz, Sarah Graham, Andreas Heil, Ben Hooker, Philipp Jager, Anita Knipper, Ephrem Mersha Wolde, Manfred Neubig, Manuel Rausch, Bernd Seeland, Cary Siress, and Marta H. Wisniewska

ETH Zurich, KIT Karlsruhe, EiABC Addis Ababa University

Marc Angélil and Cary Siress

Addis

often-questionable goals and means, whatever the rhetoric used to justify them. Conversely, any counter-imaginary concerning the more equitable restructuring of social and spatial arrangements would have to work with the base condition of hybridized territories and a hybridized socius as the initial working premise.

In the metropolitan region of Addis Ababa, the hybridization of territory comes in the form of shiny ensembles overshadowing indigenous settlements, traffic arteries disrupting the labyrinth of pedestrian paths, and agro-industries springing up next to the remnants of subsistence farms, to mention just a few of the more striking spatial juxtapositions—and all this superimposed on the residue of past layers of nation-building processes. Woven into this already complicated spatial hybrid are mixed modes of social organization (ethnic affiliations, religious groups, agricultural cooperatives, neighborhood associations, trade unions), along with various modes of production (agricultural, industrial, microentrepreneurial, service-oriented), all coexisting in fractured and multiple forms to produce a composite economy, including those practices that are considered informal. This is the terrain on which the coming iterations of Ethiopia will have to be articulated, rather than it being wished away in some blank-slate development venture or beautification scheme.

The wild hybrid that Ethiopia and its capital have become through numerous iterations under successive political and economic systems is but one case of the all-too-worldly reality that any counter-imaginary of development will have to confront anywhere on the planet, considering that Ethiopia is but one poignant iteration of a now subjugated globe.

Ababa

Cultural Resilience: Perspectives from Al Azraq Refugee Camp, Jordan

Azra Akšamija and
Melina Philippou,
MIT Future Heritage Lab

Al

The traditional ideal of living in a single-family home on privately-owned land, surrounded by neighbors of the same ethnic and economic background, is no longer tenable. Forced displacement due to conflicts, climate change, scarcity of resources and economic inequality, shape our new reality. An increasing number of people are forced to move and adapt to unexpected life scenarios.

> How can architecture respond to and shape
> this new model of life?
> What can architecture do for and learn from
> the forcefully displaced?

Only fifteen years old at the time, Mohammed initiated the first refugee-led publication of Al Azraq Refugee Camp in Jordan to support its approximately 36,000 Syrian residents. Known as the "Heartbeat of Al Azraq Camp," the magazine took off thanks to friendships that Mohammed made with twelve teenagers who landed in Azraq from other parts of Syria. Together, they defied the challenges of confinement by writing poetry and documenting their lives in short movies. Today, Mohammed and Hussein are higher education students. Since the camp has no access to accredited degrees, they commute to Amman for many hours every day. Others, like Wael and Jar, find strength and inspiration in martial arts. Jar dropped out of school. He does not see how formal education can better his future. Instead, he focuses on his own inventions: he can teach you how to mitigate the unbearable heat of the standardized shelters with desert coolers and portable fountains. Wael, the most promising graduate of Al Azraq Camp Taekwondo Academy is heading to the Tokyo Olympics.

following: Al Azraq Refugee Camp in the stony plains of the Eastern Jordanian desert is the temporary home for 36,000 Syrian refugees. The camp is located about 100 km east of Amman, and 25 km west of the town of Azraq.

With their fractured histories and hybrid identities, Mohammad, Hussein, Wael, and Jar are protagonists of a growing, global population forced to leave their homes due to conflict and crisis. Today, more than 70.8 million refugees, asylum seekers, and internally displaced persons are on the move

Azraq Camp

Azra Akšamija and Melina Philippou

Azraq Camp

Azra Akšamija and Melina Philippou

Al

Azraq Camp   31

in search of safe grounds.[1] Climate change, natural disasters, and human-made inequalities are expected to accelerate this trend: since 2008, an average of 25.3 million displacements were caused by natural disasters alone.[2]

One of the most profound challenges of displacement in contexts of conflict and crisis is the disconnection from established cultural practices, history, and identity. While the sustenance and dynamic development of culture are embedded in cities characterized by environmental, political, and financial stability through institutional and governmental pathways, displaced people in refugee camps and other emergency response schemes have very limited, if any, access to relevant cultural infrastructure. While humanitarian responses focus on supporting the basic biological needs of refugees, we argue that a focus on cultural resilience is of major importance to overcome adversity and the danger of cultural erasure, social divisions, and marginalization of populations on the move to safe grounds.

BARRIERS TO EQUITABLE CULTURAL RESILIENCE

Challenges contributing to the cultural vulnerability of the forcefully displaced refer to the destruction of heritage sites, assimilation practices, and the neglect of cultural resilience concerns in humanitarian relief.

Human-made and natural disasters that are prompting people to flee have a direct impact on monuments, sites, and landscapes of historic and cultural significance. From the weaponization of heritage destruction as part of contemporary warfare—as exemplified by the targeted destruction of Palmyra by ISIL in 2015—to the growing vulnerability of monuments due to the frequency and intensity of climate change impacts in precarious geographies, such as in Southeast Asia, the forcefully displaced are vulnerable to cultural erasure.

1   "Figures at a Glance," United Nations High Commissioner for Refugees (UNHCR), accessed April 3, 2020, https://www.unhcr.org /figures-at-a-glance.html.

2   "Disasters and Climate Change," Internal Displacement Monitoring Centre (IMDC), accessed April 3, 2020, https:// www.internal-displace ment.org/disasters -and-climate-change.

Azra Akšamija and Melina Philippou

Al

The second concern relates to the rise of cultural divides, aggravated by the biased representations of immigrants, as well as "assimilation as integration" schemes and similar policies of cultural oppression in host countries. While integration implies that individuals from different cultural milieus are to be incorporated into society as equals, assimilation, on the other hand, implies that individuals need to fully adopt the cultural norms of the dominant/host society in order to earn their place in it. The question of how displaced people relate to and become part of the host society—including the rights to presence, visibility, religious freedom, and inclusion of diversity—is tightly linked to dominant politics of identity and cultural representation.

Finally, a critical barrier to the cultural resilience of displaced people is the capacity to access means for cultural resilience during humanitarian emergencies. Policies of humanitarian relief have remained almost unchanged since the Universal Declaration of Human Rights after WWII, focusing on a "basic needs" approach and assisting with biological needs for survival such as nutrition, hygiene, and shelter.[3] Considerations of culture in humanitarian aid have emerged recently as a means to improve the psychosocial wellbeing of refugees. That said, until today humanitarian relief neglects the significance of spatial qualities for healing, community building, and cultural expression, leaving refugees subject to the continuous loss of cultural memory and identity, all of which contributes to the weakening of their social structures.

3   "The UNHCR Results Framework defines basic needs in terms of access to basic services and assistance in health, nutrition, WASH, food, shelter, energy, education, as well as domestic items and specialized services for people with specific needs." United Nations High Commissioner for Refugees, "Basic Needs Approach in the Refugee Response," UNHCR website, accessed 12 January 2021, https://www.unhcr.org/protection/operations/590aefc77/basic-needs-approach-refugee-response.html.

CHALLENGES IN REFUGEE CAMPS
The absence of cultural resilience and preservation concerns in humanitarian relief is more urgent in the case of refugee camps, especially when one takes into consideration that the median stay in protracted refugee situations is almost twenty

years.[4] Though the majority of displaced people find refuge in cities and peri-urban areas worldwide, around 40% are still living in refugee camps and other temporary spaces of confinement.[5] Challenges for cultural resilience in refugee contexts take spatial forms, starting from the marginalization of displaced people in remote settings, to the cultural deprivation of humanitarian design, and regulations that limit refugee-led interventions in the built environment of refugee camps.

Refugees follow a perilous journey through borders, transit stations, and processing centers before arriving at refugee camps, which are often situated in remote locations, away from urban environments and their supporting infrastructure. Excluded geographically, socially, and often financially from exchanges with the host community, refugees are also deprived from access to resources for community building and preservation of memory while in exile. As spaces of inscribed exclusion, refugee camps exemplify the design for "how *not* to live together" with the host community, while keeping refugees dependent on it for both material needs and identity-building.

The outputs of humanitarian design are driven by a utilitarian problem-solving approach. While camps provide physical shelter through tents, caravans, and barracks, their design often neglects the fundamental emotional, cultural, and educational needs of their residents. Traumatized from the war and stripped of their homes, history, and identity camp residents face deep challenges beyond the basic needs for food and safety. At the same time, camp legislation challenges the agency of residents to introduce their own designs in the camp. Under the guideline for the environmental sustainability of refugee camps, residents are discouraged to alter their surroundings and are prevented from introducing foundation-bearing structures.

4   United Nations High Commissioner for Refugees (UNHCR), Executive Committee of the High Commissioner's Programme, "Protracted Refugee Situations," Standing Committee, 30th Meeting, EC/54/SC/CRP.14, June 10, 2004, 2, http://www.unhcr.org/40c982172/.

5   "Refugee Facts: Refugee Camps," United Nations High Commissioner for Refugees (UNHCR), accessed April 3, 2020, https://www.unrefugees.org/refugee-facts/camps/. See also Melina Philippou, "Border as Nomos: An Alternative for the Stateless" (master's thesis, Massachusetts Institute of Technology, 2016), https://dspace.mit.edu/handle/1721.1/115014.

Azra Akšamija and Melina Philippou

For many children the corrugated steel shelters fenced in deserted landscapes become the main cultural reference. Residents of refugee camps are subjected to cultural deprivation in a state of prolonged impermanence.

Under the concern of safety, social spaces outside NGO supervision and operations are formally prohibited. With limitations on both personalizing the built environment and introducing spaces for social exchange, community building is limited to NGO programs in designated centers that operate during limited office hours.

The cultural deprivation in refugee camps is a profound challenge that raises concerns for the loss of memory and identity, as well as for the revitalization of social structures of displaced communities. Tools for cultural resilience should be equally accessible to all regardless of the geographic, financial or political geography of their country of origin. Rethinking humanitarian design from the lens of cultural resilience and transcultural understanding is thus more important than ever.

CULTURAL RESILIENCE THROUGH REFUGEE DESIGN: THE CASE OF AL AZRAQ CAMP

Established in 2014 at the stony plains of the Eastern Jordanian desert, Al Azraq Refugee Camp was founded when the country's largest refugee camp, Al Zaatari, reached its full capacity. Al Azraq was designed to be the region's largest camp with the capacity to house up to 130,000 people. Today, it is the second largest camp in the region and the temporary home for more than 36,000 Syrian refugees, living in thousands of identical 28m² corrugated steel shelters. Inhabitants are confronted with the challenges of containment, geographic isolation, extreme weather conditions, and scarcity. On entry, one encounters the securitization of camp management, enforced by the Jordanian police, and the constraints of containment. Mobility between the camp and the rest of the world is contingent upon shifting bureaucratic schemes governed by a humanitarian-military nexus. The sense of confinement and isolation

following: During the summer, temperatures in the corrugated metal sheet caravans can reach over 45°C.

Azraq Camp

Azra Akšamija and Melina Philippou

Al

Azraq Camp

intensifies in view of the barren landscape, evidence of the hostile living conditions.

Syrian refugees contest the camp austerity. Standardized designs aiming to serve the mere biological needs of the body, are supplemented with personalized design interventions across scales.[6] These range from ornaments made from date seeds, to improvised fountains of shisha components, kitchen extensions with metal scraps for baking goods, and street designs for the privacy of extended families. These interventions are expressions of the camp residents' aesthetic and cultural needs, personal tastes, and forms of play. They generate a new set of relations, events, and rituals in the camp that reflect on life before war, while contributing to the preservation of the living culture at present.

6 Giorgio Agamben, *Homo Sacer: Sovereign Power and Bare Life*, trans. Daniel Heller-Roazen (Stanford, CA: Stanford University Press, 1998), 95–102.

Glass and porcelain cups of this tea set are covered with a veneer of date seeds. Date seeds are easy to find at the camp as they are disposed during the date-molasses-making process. Each seed is carved and polished into sections. Then the seeds are arranged to form different patterns on the cup using a combination of brown or white adhesive. The white adhesive is a mix of glue and powdered milk, and the brown adhesive is mixed from coffee and glue.

Azra Akšamija and Melina Philippou

Made out of everyday household items, this fountain is easy to assemble and turn back into parts without destroying its components: a set of buckets, yogurt containers, shisha parts, and a motor make up its parts.

Azraq Camp

A number of traditional dishes of the Syrian cuisine require baking and roasting in an oven. Because ovens are not considered a Core Relief Item, one resident made one for his family reusing multiple metal scraps from the walls of the shelter. The oven is attached to a gas can.

Azra Akšamija and Melina Philippou

The gate signifies the transition from the village to a collective open space resilient to flooding. The residents of the plot introduced paving, porches, and a canopy of thermal blankets.

Azraq Camp 41

Desert Castle

The desert castles of Al Azraq Camp disrupt the repetition of standardized T-shelters. The life-sized adobe structures reference the history of Syria and Jordan–the Arch of Triumph in Palmyra, the citadel of Aleppo, and the Umayyad desert palaces of the Eastern Jordanian desert located a few miles away. They contrast the ahistoric and culturally deprived camp landscape. Overcoming the austerity of the camp, the designer of the *Desert Castle* employed the few materials found on site: stones, sand, and metal sheets scraps from deserted shelters. As for the building regulations of the camp, *Desert Castles* are considered clay sculptures. By registering as "sculptures" rather than "monuments," these structures surpass the prohibition on refugee-led permanent buildings. A landmark and social space for residents, and humanitarian workers, the castle was soon destroyed by the elements of nature. The *Desert Castles* of Al Azraq camp reappropriated the desert from a symbol of isolation to a medium for cultural expression, the dynamic development of culture, and the negotiation of identity.

Majlis

With public spaces outside NGO-designated land being regulated, the *Majlis* tradition contributes to the preservation of memory by enabling social gatherings of the community.[7] The U-shaped, floor-level seating areas for communal events in dedicated shelters in the camp are an informal setting for community gatherings led by refugees themselves. The shelter interior is retrofitted to represent their important role in the village. The design adds an aesthetic value to the function of Core Relief Items (CRI).[8] The side walls are decorated with painted murals of ancient ruins. The ceiling is upholstered with CRI distributed in winter months. A plastic sheet is draped towards the side sections and a thermal blanket runner follows the roof ridge. The center wall is covered with multiple layers of fabric.

7 *Majlis* is an Arabic and Persian term denoting a council, a space for the gathering of administrative, religious and social groups. In private spaces, the term denotes spaces for welcoming guests, equivalent to a living room.

8 Core Relief Items (CRI) refers to aid essentials, distributed to refugees by humanitarian NGOs upon arrival and periodically within the year. CRI include thermal blankets, insulation sheets, sleeping mats, tarpaulins, and jerry cans.

Azra Akšamija and Melina Philippou

"Human beings are made of clay too. Allah took some clay and made us out of it, so we have an eternal empathy to the ground. Now there's cement. The world changed. Sobhan Allah," says Abu Ali, a carpenter and construction worker who built this sculpture reminiscent of the Palmyra Arch. He is well known at the camp for his sand castles. Today, he works at the camp market selling mobile phones and accessories.

For Abu Mohamad, the eldest in the neighborhood, a Majlis is "a symbol of Arab hospitality." Gatherings break the social isolation of people in the camp, engaging them in informal conversations. Abu Mohamad explains that when people from different age groups and backgrounds meet, they learn from each other's life experiences, and combat loneliness through communion.

Azraq Camp 43

Azra Akšamija and Melina Philippou

Al

The composition includes thermal blankets, prayer rugs, and fabric from the local market. Floor and back cushions are made out of sleeping mats, upholstered with thermal blankets and lined with orange fabric scraps. The floor is covered with colorful tarpaulins. The coffee table is, at any time, prepared for serving. Gatherings break the isolation of people engaging them in open conversations. It is a space for exchange across generations, ethnicity, and gender or as the host shares "*Al Majalis Madaris*," translating to "The *Majlis* [gatherings] are schools." Given the lack of formal pathways for education on Syrian history and the preservation of memory, the *Majlis* are an open invitation to learn from a conversation, a poem, a story.

Pigeon Lofts

Crossing the camp one observes pigeon flocks in beautiful formations close to the shelters. Known as urban species, one wonders about their presence in the desert. The collection, capturing, breeding, and flying of pigeons is a popular hobby in Syria that refugees brought with them to the camp. The high border walls and deep cooing sounds coming from the pigeon lofts on the side of the shelter entrance build an alternate world. Pigeon breeders alter the roof with the addition of a landing board and the facade of the structure with the attachment of pigeon lofts. The landing board frame is covered with a net knit from laundry rope. The board is placed on top of several burlap sheets layered to reduce landing noise in the shelter interior. The pigeon lofts have wooden frames covered with IBR metal sheet walls and plastic sheet curtain rollers. They have multiple pens with different roles. The smaller pens protect hatching and the squabs until they are ready to fly, while the larger pens serve the separation of female and male pigeons at times. In a place like Azraq, where resources are scarce, pigeon keeping is about the camaraderie of a like-minded community and the continuation of everyday practices reminiscent of home.

"It is beautiful to raise pigeons. When I fly the flock I forget all of my worries. Their spirit resonates with people. Pigeons understand pride. It is a prestigious sport. Doctors and Lawyers raise pigeons and Kings used to do it as well," says Amer, who grew up in a household of pigeon fanciers. He was taught how to breed pigeons by his siblings. He has been pursuing pigeon keeping for more than twelve years.

Azraq Camp

45

The interventions of Syrian refugees at Al Azraq camp, unearth the deep desire for cultural expression in conditions of forced displacement and suggest a humanitarian design approach for the cultural resilience of vulnerable communities in refugee spaces. The interventions of Syrian refugees offer culturally specific and environmentally sustainable alternatives to standardized design of humanitarian shelters. Refugee-led interventions demonstrate aesthetic quality and social relevance, with the potential to capture, sustain, and advance the living culture of threatened communities through creative interpretations of historical and cultural forms. Cultural preservation in conditions of forced displacement according to refugee designs points towards an increased valorization of social objectives, from an institutional to a bottom-up approach.

CULTURE IS AN ESSENTIAL HUMAN NEED!

What can the field of architecture learn from the refugee-led design cultural interventions in Al Azraq Refugee Camp?

While humanitarian responses center their efforts on the basic biological needs of refugees, focusing on cultural resilience is of major importance to overcome adversity and the danger of cultural erasure, social divisions, and marginalization. Humanitarian design today is not equipped to meet the cultural needs of a continuously increasing displaced population and address the pressing concerns of their cultural survival. Thus, rethinking humanitarian design from the lens of cultural resilience is more critical than ever.

By enabling the enactment of cultural practices at Al Azraq Camp, cultural interventions by

PROJECT CREDITS

Azra Akšamija, Melina Philippou, Zeid Madi, and Raafat Majzoub with Residents/designers at Al Azraq Camp: *Abu Jar Al Ajnabi, Majid Sa'man Al Halipha, Amer Yassin Abu Haitham, Abu Mohammad Al Homsani, Majid Al Kan'an, Ali Fawaz, Mohammed Khaled Marzouqi, Abdel Rachman, Farez Jamel Vousel*; Residents/ authors of poems and stories at Al Azraq Camp: *Heba Al Saleh, Nagham Al Saleh, Nour Ghassan, Samer Al-Naser, Hana'a Ahmed, Kifah Akeel, Hussein Al-Abdallah, Hasan Al-Abdallah, Hatem Al-Balkhy, Wa'el Al-Faraj, Nagham Alsalha, Heba Caleh, Mohammed Al-Hamedy, Ahma Al-Hassan, Jar Al-Naby Abazaid,*

Azra Akšamija and Melina Philippou

Al

Syrian refugees provide valuable models for architects and humanitarians for how to design and build cultural resilience during humanitarian emergencies. These designs call our attention to:

Yassin Al-Yassin, Mustafa Hamadah, Jameel Homede, Abdulkarim Ihsan, Ahmad Khalaf, Rawan Maher Hossin, Mohamed Mez'al, Jameel Mousli, Mohammed Shaban; Photographic survey of inventions: Zeid Madi, Nabil Sayfayn Al Azraq Journal team members: Mohammad Al Qo'airy, Hussain Al Abdullah, Yassin Al Yassin, Jameel Homede, Mohamed Mez'al; Advisors in German Jordanian University, Amman: Rejan Ashour, Mohammad Yaghan

The findings presented in this paper build on multiannual research conducted by various researchers and collaborators of the MIT Future Heritage Lab

1. The value of social objectives linked to cultural preservation in crisis zones;
2. The necessity to rethink humanitarian design beyond the basic needs approach, towards the acceptance of cultural expression as an essential human need;
3. The agency of art and design in developing new tools for the capturing, maintenance, and dynamic development of cultural practices of displaced people.

Building capacity for cultural resilience in refugee camps is about providing the means for the dynamic preservation of social relations and networks of communities in threat. Using artistic methods, critical design tools, transdisciplinary processes, and sustainable materials, the lessons from refugee designs have the potential to impact established approaches in heritage preservation and humanitarian design and have a wide-reaching impact on displaced communities.

Azraq Camp

Beirut Shifting Grounds

Sandra Frem and Boulos Douaihy

> "The value of cities is determined according to the number of places where improvisation is permitted."
> —Siegfried Kracauer, *Streets in Berlin & Elsewhere*

CREATIVE OR DESTRUCTIVE CHAOS?

Beirut's constant revival in the face of never-ending political dysfunction appears to have finally ended last year... with a bang. The blast that pulverized the Port of Beirut on August 4, 2020 was felt as far as Cyprus. Caused by a stockpile of unsafely stored ammonium nitrate that laid there in full knowledge of the authorities, it devastated large parts of the city, left thousands of people homeless, in addition to a heavy death and casualty toll.[1] As one of the biggest non-nuclear explosions in history, the blast was one of many intersecting disasters last year in Beirut generated by the country's failed governance.

After the events of 2020, Beirut's branded "creative chaos" can hardly be romanticized; the meltdown of its financial and banking sectors, paired with the domination of a corrupt and incompetent political elite, has led the country to collapse.[2]

Beirut is now a tired city in desperate need of a promise of a different course, one of stability and collective reclamation.

A FAILED SYSTEM

The economic and political systems that have governed Beirut since the end of the Lebanese Civil War went to extremes in favoring the private and marginalizing the public.

These systems find their roots in a social pact that tied communal representation to sectarian identity, at the dawn of the country's independence in the forties. This construct installed an entrenched culture of clientelism and corruption that pervaded

1   See Forensic Architecture and Mada Masr, "Investigation: The Beirut Port Explosion," Forensic Architecture, November 17, 2020, https://forensic-architecture.org/investigation/beirut-port-explosion.

2   Hannes Baumann, "Lebanon's Economic Crisis Didn't Happen Overnight. So How Did It Get to this Point?" *The Washington Post*, October 22, 2019, https://www.washingtonpost.com/politics/2019/10/22/lebanons-economic-crisis-didnt-happen-overnight-so-how-did-it-get-this-point/.

Beirut cityscape showing Martyrs' Square in the city's downtown area.

rut

Sandra Frem and Boulos Douaihy

Bei

My Government Did This, *View of the Beirut Port after the August 4, 2020 blast.*

state institutions, bureaucracies and infrastructures, leading after several decades to economic bankruptcy and the failure to deliver the most basic services.[3]

This system extended into the physical realm, manifesting in the quasi-nonexistence of public spaces in Beirut—a public domain that is continuously and casually aggressed by the private[4]— as well as the dysfunction of public buildings that reflect the chronic weakness of the state.[5]

The *laissez-faire* culture allowed political powers, in partnership with private interests, to feed off the public realm by suffocating the skies, eating up the remaining lots and appropriating the sea with numerous infringements— from adopting toxic landfills to acquiring more shore for development, by any means necessary.

In short, the kleptocracy ate up the public realm.

Opportunism

On the ground, the neoliberal logics of capital reshaped the interface between private and public, converting the urban experience of Beirut's groundscape to a question of property ownership.[6] Ground became a base for investment, and its worth equated its vertical FAR.

Guided by an intentionally loose building code, profit-driven construction damaged the city's physiognomy with the proliferation of towers that disfigured preexisting topography and skyline alike.[7]

The construction spree portrayed the archaic culture that ruled and ruined the city. Empty and unfinished projects stand today throughout Beirut as the ultimate representation of this failed system that rested too much and for too long on real-estate investment as a cornerstone for the economy.

3   Rebecca Collard, "How Sectarianism Helped Destroy Lebanon's Economy," *Foreign Policy*, December 13, 2019, https://foreign policy .com/2019/12/13 /sectarianism-helped -destroy-lebanon -economy/.

4   While the coastline is protected by law from private ownership and construction, very few accesses to the sea remain public. See Habib Battah, "The Fencing of Dalieh," *Beirut Report*, June 6, 2014, http://www .beirutreport.com/2014 /06/the-fencing-of -dalieh.html.

5   Carla Aramouny, "Electricité du Liban: A Landmark from Beirut's 'Golden Age' of Modern Architecture," *Brownbook Magazine*, no. 66 (2017): 64–77.

6   The postwar boom in real estate led to a massive destruction of the urban fabric, resulting in gated high-rises in different neighborhoods. See Marieke Krijnen, *Conference Report: Creative Economy, Social Justice, and Urban Strategies: The Case of Mar Mikhael* (Beirut:

Issam Fares Institute for Public Policy and International Affairs, American University of Beirut, 2016).

7   Private development reduced the city's open spaces to a mere 600,000 m², less than 5% of its overall area. See Samir Khalaf, "Post-War Barbarism in Lebanon," *An-Nahar*, February 22, 2019, https://en .annahar.com/article /940004-postwar -barbarism-in-lebanon/.

8   Mona Fawaz, Mona Harb, and Ahmad Gharbieh, "Living Beirut's Security Zones: An Investigation of the Modalities and Practice of Urban Security," *City & Society* 24, no. 2 (August 2012): 173–95.

9   While the coastline is protected by law from private ownership and construction, very few accesses to the sea remain public. See Habib Battah, "A City Without a Shore: Rem Koolhaas, Dalieh and the Paving of Beirut's Coast," *The Guardian*, March 17, 2015, https:// www.theguardian.com /cities/2015/mar/17 /rem-koolhaas-dalieh -beirut-shore-coast.

At the scale of the building, the *Beirut Shifting Grounds* project at La Biennale di Venezia's 17th International Architecture Exhibition magnifies the architecture of the ground through a comparative outlook of sectional relationships where buildings engage the public ground of Beirut. In a city where the ground has been shaped by its urban architecture rather than by its planning, we look at the different architectures that largely shaped the city through different periods, drawing connections between the regulations that produced them and the type of public grounds they helped create.

Restriction

As a reflection of political oligarchy and unbridled capitalism, Beirut's ground has been transformed into a complicit agent of control, embedding values such as militarization, security and exclusivity.[8] Boundaries and borders are persistent elements that punctuate the urban landscape, fencing off private as well as public properties, and creating the latent experience of restricted access.[9] However, restriction went to new extremes in 2020; the first pandemic lockdown in March of that year prohibited being in public space, coinciding in time to crush the critical mass of public dissent that had taken to the streets since October 17, 2019. Later on, the mounting health and financial crises quashed people's experience of the public ground altogether. Open spaces were restricted, banks and other financial and public institutions became barricaded, commercial streets and malls were emptied as purchasing power dwindled down with the simultaneous devaluation of the currency and soaring of prices, leaving Beirut in arrested development—in what feels like a financial, mental, and physical exile from the rest of the world.

As a response to such ground conditions, our project presents a series of human-scale installations designed by architecture students at the American University of Beirut (AUB) as part of a research studio course called *BePublic* that recurred over the span of two decades. They are discursive, often ironic, interventions that critique the existing subversive practices of Beirut's ground. These micro architectures have been plugged into different parts of the city and specifically in locations where the public's access is unreasonably denied.[10] Each project is a statement that comments on the boundaries that cripple the public's engagement with the city, whose effects ripple regardless of its ephemeral nature. *Dare to Approach, Sma3 La Farjik, Tashwish,* and *Air Rights* are a few examples that resulted from using situated installations in public space as a pedagogical tool to create a dialogue between people and their surroundings.[11]

THE PROACTIVE GROUND
Improvisation

Throughout the past decades, lacking public services have prompted a counterculture of improvisation in Beirut that defined the character of its citizens and its civic organizations. Such practices are proof of the inventiveness and self-organization that spilled to the built environment.

From alternative services by private providers, to food banks and social services of an active NGO scene, to the solidary behaviors of citizens when encountering hardship, such practices came to define the experience of the city and its ground, making it vibrant and, at times, benevolent despite its adversities.

As the embodiment of this experience, Beirut's urban patchworks gave room to the

10 BePublic is a research lab that stems from a series of public installations with a short life span. More information on the lab's website, https://www.aub.edu.lb/msfea/research/Pages/be-public.aspx.

11 *Dare to Approach.* Designers: Amina Kassem, Sari el Kantari, Elie Geha, Tamara Salloum. Studio: Bepublic/Appropriation 2018. Conducted by Rana Haddad and Pascal Hachem at the American University of Beirut. *Sma3 La Farjik.* Designers: Nadine Abdulsalam, Faisal Annab, Racha Doughman, Nadine Eid, Lea Ramadan. Studio: Bepublic/Silence 2016. Conducted by Rana Haddad and Joanne Hayek at the American University of Beirut. *Tashwish.* Designers: Betina Abi Habib, Zeina Bekhaazi, Souha Boumatar, Mario El Khouri, Karen Madi. Studio: Bepublic/Silence 2016. Conducted by Rana Haddad and Joanne Hayek at the American University of Beirut. *Air Rights.* Designers: Youssef Ibrahim, Jana Aridi, Loulwa Achkar, Thea Hallak, Micheline Nahra. Studio: Bepublic/Public Beirut 2012. Conducted by Rana Haddad, Carole Levesque, and Sandra Richani at the American University of Beirut.

BePublic installations,
a pedagogical tool
to engage with the
built environment:
In Between *(above),*
Listen to Observe *(right).*

Appropriations as a new
aesthetic of the ground.

Sandra Frem and Boulos Douaihy

Bei

Beirut rhythms and
multiplicities.

Typologies of boundaries

barricading downtown

Beirut.

Sandra Frem and Boulos Douaihy

many rhythms and multiplicities that are found in its diverse urban fabric.

Often nested in "third spaces" at the intersection of private and public realms, spontaneous appropriations overlay the ground to accommodate people's mixed activities and living needs, like grocer's crates on the sidewalks serving as the make-shift porch of a "mini-market"; a sidewalk turning into a temporary playground; and improvised seating that transforms the ground into an outdoor living room.

The varying levels of appropriations imbue the ground with a sense of legibility—and arguably, an identity—that the built form fails to deliver. In their informality, such ephemeral expressions define a new aesthetic of the ground, transforming it into a supportive realm where life is bound to assert itself.

Such acts of small-scale takeover acquired national proportions in the brief period that preceded the 2020 meltdown, with the massive reclamation of public space that was sparked by the October 17th Revolution.

In our project, we explore this ambivalent relationship between the architecture of the ground and its appropriation in seven examples from different Beiruti neighborhoods: Achrafieh (Sassine), Badaro, Mar Mikhael, Bourj Hammoud (Nor Marash), Hamra, Jnah, and Ain El Remmane. In each of them, we look at the urban and social porosities between street space and private properties that give rise to localized practices, spatial appropriations, and coping mechanisms.

Reclamation

The October 17th Revolution caught the Lebanese by surprise. Not for a lack of good reasons to revolt, given high levels of unemployment, poverty, and discontent with state governance, but for the sudden awakening of multiple generations that simultaneously took to the streets to demand the dissolution of the government regardless of political or sectarian affiliations.[12] The most unanticipated element was, perhaps, the demand for basic human rights after years of internalized injustice, such as the right to public space, for people to

12 "Lebanon Protests Explained," Amnesty International, updated September 22, 2020, https://www.amnesty.org/en/latest/news/2019/11/lebanon-protests-explained/.

rut

reclaim the city as their own. This motivation translated into innovative occupations of the public realm in the weeks that followed the initial mass protests.[13]

The widespread social uprising started in Beirut but rapidly spread to every city in the country, resulting in the occupation of roads and squares across Lebanon on the night of October 17, 2019. Over several months, grassroots protests submerged the city's streets, reconnecting people—through public use—with Beirut's public ground and becoming a form of resistance to systems of political and spatial dominion. People protested present conditions and imagined alternative futures in the public space. Everywhere, new commons emerged, reclaiming the roads, roundabouts, and urban voids that were lost to cars and bad governance in decades past. During this period of contestation and activism, one of the most noteworthy reclamations was the reactivation, through spontaneous occupation, of forgotten and often abandoned landmarks and places that came to symbolize social and spatial alienation in the last few decades.

The infamous Ring Road that separates downtown Beirut from the rest of the city was dubbed as بيت الشعب, "House of the People," and hosted versatile programs around the clock. Abandoned buildings that were left to ruin under Solidere—the private real estate company that was in charge of the reconstruction of downtown Beirut after the Lebanese Civil War (1975–1990)—such as the Grand Theater and the Beirut City Center (colloquially known as The Egg) were rediscovered by the people and became symbols of the revolution. Manicured open spaces of Solidere that used to be mostly empty, such as the Gibran Khalil Gibran and Samir Kassir gardens, became places for dynamic gatherings, talks, and debates.

Many roads leading to city's downtown became pedestrian, and people revived the act of being and walking in spaces they had only ever crossed by car.

13 See Kareem Chehayeb, "Beirut's Protest City Is a Rebuke to the Privatization of Public Space," *Bloomberg CityLab*, October 31, 2019, https://www.bloomberg.com/news/articles/2019-10-31/beirut-s-protesters-assert-their-right-to-the-city, and Antoine Atallah, "Reclaiming the City…Another Win for the Thawra," *L'Orient Le Jour*, December 9, 2019, https://www.lorientlejour.com/article/1197926/reclaiming-the-city-another-win-for-the-thawra.html/.

Sandra Frem and Boulos Douaihy

*above: October 17th
Revolution.*

*right: Reclamation of
the abandoned Grand
Theater in downtown
Beirut during the
October 17th Revolution.*

Martyrs' Square emerged as a miniature city, with a stage zone for large gatherings, makeshift tents for debates, areas for recreation, communal kitchens, portable toilets and even kids' spaces. The street that links the square to the Riad Al-Solh Square was converted into an open-air food market, and the latter became an outdoor forum for discussions. For the first time in decades, people protested, chanted, marched, sat down, talked, ate, gathered, and debated in the public realm. Anyone could access downtown Beirut. Daily soup kitchens invited a long-shunned underprivileged group to the space. Cart vendors flocked back downtown after decades of being banned to access that part of town. The area recovered its pre-war name *al-balad*, and with it, assumed a role during the first months of the revolution that is not far from when it was indeed a popular destination for all factions of society.

These spatial settings encouraged an open and flexible system while allowing people to use the space in unpredictable ways. The emerging public realm was a result of community actions and negotiations that did not escape arguments and tensions, but that could still be interpreted positively since those using the space were creating innovative approaches to communal life.

Over three months of "occupation," new social and spatial practices emerged in line with the growing collective identity, evident numerous initiatives that "nurtured" the reclaimed public realm, through grassroots governance and innovative programming.

The people took up the mantel of the government, providing basic services: cleaning and waste recycling campaigns were held daily by volunteers; psychological and social aid was offered; open classrooms were held in certain tents. Education was brought to the street, where university professors, lawyers, activists and the general public suggested and debated solutions to the crisis in a non-hierarchical manner. Such practices were accompanied by a network of grassroots organizations outside the influence of the political establishment and built, through their actions, alternative values of citizenry. Simultaneously, independent journalism

Sandra Frem and Boulos Douaihy

Bei

platforms emerged and contributed—for the first time—to an informed public.[14]

The revolution adopted networked organizational structures between the different groups and was deliberately leaderless, as a critique to the sectarian *zaim*, the parochial figure of the leader that always monopolized political representation in Lebanon.

In this period, downtown Beirut became what Richard Sennett describes in his book *Uses of Disorder* as a lesson for urban planners—an unregulated public space where people learn how to tolerate difference, which encourages social interaction and the emergence of unplanned activities.[15]

Regardless of the revolution's outcomes, of its successes or failures, the spatial appropriation and social solidarity that were enacted in the public realm in this period taught citizens about the latent potentials of their urban space and their capacities within collective space-making, valuable precedents for the future use and planning of urban spaces in Beirut.

For our project, we look at the ground through time, unfolding the genealogy of the city's prime space—Martyrs' Square—the fluctuation of its identity, urban form, and "publicness" from the Ottoman period to the October 17th Revolution. We trace its evolution into a prominent national space of social and political significance, foregrounding how its ground allowed for different communal expressions throughout history.

Production

The economic crisis in Lebanon is one of a country that was led by its successive governments to live well beyond its means, with a linear economy that relied on imports and the accumulation of debt.[16] The resultant consumptive pace had a heavy ecological, social, and spatial footprint, encouraging a frivolous preference of foreign imports over local

14 They include, among many others not mentioned here: Beirut Madinati, Beit El Baraka, Offrejoie, The Volunteer Circle, Daleel Thawra, Lebanon Support, Muwatn Libnan, Nawaya Network, as well as independent media outlets, such as Megaphone and the Beirut Report.

15 Richard Sennett, *The Uses of Disorder: Personal Identity and City Life* (New York, Knopf, 1970).

16 See TK Maloy, "IIF: The Origins of Lebanon's Economic Crisis," *An-nahar*, February 28, 2020, https://www.annahar .com/english/article /1133102-iif-the -origins-of-lebanons -economic-crisis.

production and creating deep inequalities across sectors and regions in Lebanon, more specifically between Beirut and its hinterland.

This all came to a halt with the devaluation and hyper-inflation of the local currency in early 2020, with most of the urban population working for salaries that have lost over half of their value in the black market. The extended COVID-19 lockdown and rising prices of 85% of staple goods coincided with the self-isolation of many urban dwellers in the country-side and led to the reemergence of local production and farm-ing as a mean to curb food insecurity and cope with the crisis.[17]

During this period, for many people, agriculture became a means to tend to their needs and achieve food indepen-dence, away from market fluctuations. This revived agrarian practices in suburbs, villages, and abandoned lots of the hinterland, relinking rural production with the urban core, not as a less-desirable option but as an essential asset for survival. Most importantly, this "return to the roots" was not limited to the countryside; it also changed the land use of many residual open spaces in Beirut. Encouraged by multiple civil society groups and municipal initiatives that distributed free seeds and farming essentials, agriculture populated private balconies, roofs, threshold spaces and leftover lots within neighborhoods' inner fabrics.

This phenomenon came with simultaneous shifts that revived local production in other sectors: the rise of local industry as a result of an increased demand, the flexible work patterns dictated by the pandemic that allowed closer work-live loops to take place in outskirts of Beirut for the first time, and most importantly, the grassroots-initiated relief and rebuilding efforts that drove the reconstruction process after the port blast.

In their different manifestations, these trans-formations echo the nascent ethos of a grassroots culture that could reorient lifestyles, productive cycles, and the use of land towards a more local, self-sufficient, and circular metabolism in Beirut.

17 Jenny Gustafsson, "'Money Is Worth Nothing Now': How Lebanon Is Finding a Future in Farming," *The Guardian*, September 25, 2020, https://www.the guardian.com/global -development/2020/ sep/25/money-is-worth -nothing-now-how -lebanon-is-finding-a -future-in-farming.

Sandra Frem and Boulos Douaihy

Bei

left : collective custody of public space through volunteer-led waste management during the October 17th Revolution.

bottom: Producing the Ground: revival of urban agriculture after real estate crash on empty lots in Sin El Fil, Eastern suburb of Beirut.

Visible Security Mechanisms in Municipal Beirut

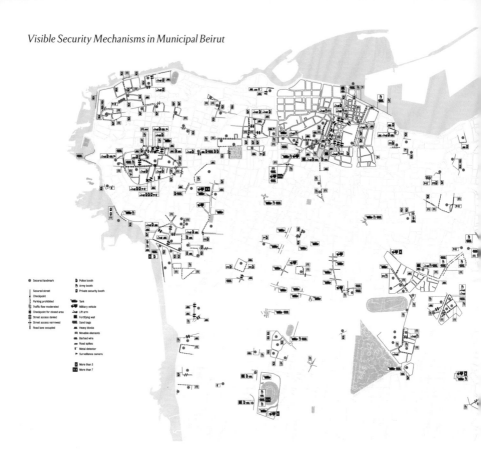

Urban Grounds Typologies

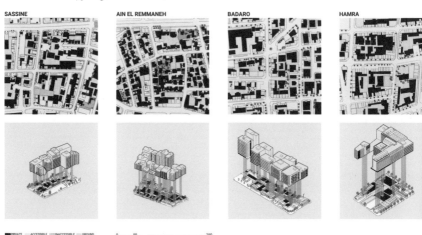

SASSINE   AIN EL REMMANEH   BADARO   HAMRA

Sandra Frem and Boulos Douaihy

Bei

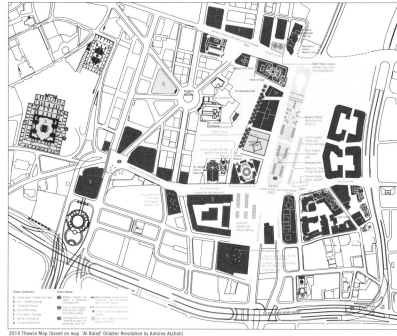

2019 Thawra Map (based on map 'Al Balad' October Revolution by Antoine Atallah)

HAMRA

BOURJ HAMMOUD (MARASH)

MAR MIKHAEL

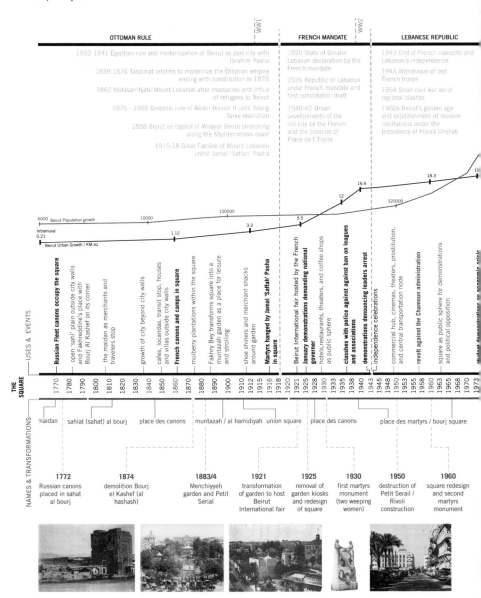

OTTOMAN RULE | WWI | FRENCH MANDATE | WW2 | LEBANESE REPUBLIC

1832-1841 Egyptian rule and modernization of Beirut as port city with Ibrahim Pasha
1839-1876 Tanzimat reforms to modernize the Ottoman empire ending with constitution in 1876
1860 Mutasarrifyate Mount Lebanon after massacres and influx of refugees to Beirut
1876 - 1909 Despotic rule of Abdul Hamid II until Young Turks revolution
1888 Beirut as capital of Wilayat Beirut stretching along the Mediterranean coast
1915-18 Great Famine of Mount Lebanon under Jamal 'Saffah' Pasha

1920 State of Greater Lebanon declaration by the French mandate
1926 Republic of Lebanon under French mandate and first constitution draft
1930-40 Urban developments of the old city by the French and the creation of Place de L'Etoile

1943 End of French mandate and Lebanon's independence
1946 Withdrawal of last French troops
1958 Short civil war amid regional clashes
1960s Beirut's golden age and establishment of modern institutions under the presidency of Fouad Chehab

6000 Beirut Population growth
Intramural 0.21
Beirut Urban Growth / KM.sq

10000
1.12

100000
3.3

5.5

12

16.4

320000

18.3

USES & EVENTS

Russian Fleet canons occupy the square
open 'sahl' plain outside city walls and Fakhreddine's place with Bourj Al Kashef on its corner
the maidan as merchants and travelers stop
growth of city beyond city walls
cafes, locandas, transit stop, houses and villas outside city walls
French canons and camps in square
mulberry plantations within the square
Fakhry Bey transforms square into a muntazah garden as a place for leisure and strolling
shoe shiners and merchant shacks around garden
Martyrs hanged by Jamal 'Saffah' Pasha in square
Beirut International fair hosted by the French
January demonstrations demanding national governer
hotels,restaurants, theaters, and coffee shops as public sphere
clashes with police against against ban on leagues and associations
demonstrations denouncing leaders arrest
Independence celebrations
commercial hub, cinemas, theaters, prostitution, and central transportation node
revolt against the Chamoun administration
square as public sphere for demonstrations and political oppostion

THE SQUARE
1770 1780 1790 1800 1810 1820 1830 1840 1850 1860 1870 1880 1890 1900 1910 1912 1915 1916 1918 1920 1921 1925 1928 1930 1933 1935 1938 1940 1943 1945 1948 1950 1953 1955 1958 1960 1963 1965 1968 1970 1973

NAMES & TRANSFORMATIONS

maidan | sahlat (sahat) al bourj | place des canons | muntazah / al hamidiyah | union square | place des canons | place des martyrs / bourj square

1772 Russian canons placed in sahat al bourj

1874 demolition Bourj el Kashef (al hashash)

1883/4 Menchiyyeh garden and Petit Serial

1921 transformation of garden to host Beirut International fair

1925 removal of garden kiosks and redesign of square

1930 first martyrs monument (two weeping women)

1950 destruction of Petit Serail / Rivoli construction

1960 square redesign and second martyrs monument

Sandra Frem and Boulos Douaihy

Bei

October 17 revolution

2000000

1500000

1200000

Greater Beirut expansion

August 4 Beirut port blast and city wide devastation and heavy human toll

Diab government resignation

square at center of conflict with snipers at the demarcation line between east and west Beirut

demolition of some destroyed buildings around the square during hopeful reconstruction efforts

tabula rasa after beirut wide demolitions

first Fairuz concert on the square after the end of war

Solidere commences post war reconstruction

square as empty road and parking intersection

Souk el barghout fair as public space activator

Solidere international competition for redesign of square

Cedar revolution and massive demonstrations against Syrian occupation

square as space for political demonstrations and sit - ins

trash crisis demonstrations & You Stink movement

the square reclaimed as public sphere, vendors, debate tents and performances

independence day celebrations on square by the people

August 4 blast and resulting mass demonstrations

1976 1977 1978 1979 1980 1981 1982 1983 1984 1985 1986 1987 1988 1989 1990 1991 1992 1993 1994 1995 1996 1997 1998 1999 2000 2001 2002 2003 2004 2005 2006 2007 2008 2009 2010 2011 2012 2013 2014 2015 2016 2017 2018 2019   2020   2021

demarcation space   martyrs square   freedom square   al saha

1975	1983	1994	2004	2005-08	2019	2020
vy war toll n square buildings	first demolition and reconstruction efforts after truce	major demolitions by Solidere of remaining buildings	re-installation of martyrs monument	March 14 cedar revolution / Hariri tomb and sit-ins	October 17 revolution and return of the square as a collective ground	August 4 damages, demonstrations, and relief grounds

AN OPPORTUNITY

If Beirut is to truly "rise from its ashes"—after the blast and throughout the ongoing health and economic crisis— it will need a new social and *spatial contract*, one that moves away from its confessional system and towards a state of pluralism, from a market-led city to a city of human-centered neighborhoods.

The crisis brings with it many opportunities. The political and economic changes that led the country to crisis are also the ones that allowed an emerging civic consciousness to challenge sectarian logics and capitalist models of development.

The reconstruction process after the blast showed first and foremost the potential of people, activists, collectives, and civil society groups in the production of the city in response to people's needs. People have learnt a lot from their most recent protest days, from their rituals under austerity and lockdown, and from the ongoing reconstruction in the destroyed neighborhoods of Beirut—albeit the need to be proactive remains in growing the positive change they aspire to. Now that Beirut is starting a new chapter, we propose different ways of inhabiting and reclaiming it, ways that reflect such aspirations and engage its realities.

Inspired by the dynamics of Beirut's collectives, we propose making use of vacant lots, structures, and existing open spaces for collective appropriation. In such realms, essential infrastructure outlets—water, electricity, data— can overlay the ground and support collective activities and exchanges, like communal kitchens, markets, temporary gatherings, and occupation. Coming from neighborhood-harnessed renewable energies, like rainwater collection and photovoltaics, such outlets can be customized, relocated, and adjusted as needed, and will be the objects of negotiation between the different collectives using it, not unlike the revolution and post-blast deployments. With the collective infrastructure serving as a supportive "carpet," we show multiple possibilities for how the ground floor could transform into an assemblage of amenities that support collective urban life.

Sandra Frem and Boulos Douaihy

Bei

About the project

Beirut Shifting Grounds is a research project that probes spatial practices of the ground level of the city that allow people to adapt through uncertainty and change. Through four parallel narratives, we focus on manifestations of improvisation, appropriation, and self-organization that offer lessons in communal adaptation and solidarity for the uncertain future.

At the human scale, we present five short films that encounter the act of "being" in Beirut's public realm through shifting conditions: privatization, political control, pandemic, and post-disaster destruction.

At the urban scale, we project the life of seven neighborhoods in Beirut through transitional moments: pre-revolution (October 2019), pre-lockdown (March 2020), and post-blast (September 2020), highlighting the transformation of each ground occupation, socio-economic conditions, and coping mechanisms.

We emphasize the importance of urban space to adapt through centuries of transition and cater to collective expressions through a time-lapse of Martyrs' Square, focusing on the evolution of its identity, urban form, and the activities it hosted.

At the architectural scale, we narrate the change brought to the built environment through specific buildings and typologies of sections that shaped the city's ground, and reflect on the reconstruction models that reshaped Beirut until the recent blast.

PROJECT CREDITS

Sandra Frem and

Boulos Douaihy with

Carla Aramouny,

Rana Haddad, and

Nicolas Fayad

American University

of Beirut

We end with an open speculation on architecture's proclivity to accommodate improvisation and offer the possibility of a city that still belongs to its inhabitants, amid shifting conditions.

Unsettled Urbanism: Hong Kong Protests in 2019

香港抗爭2019:
變動中的城市
Sampson Wong
and Merve Bedir

Hong

Since June 2019, the beginning of the Hong Kong protests, the tram stops on Hong Kong Island have undergone a profound transformation, making them the city's most important site for political graffiti. Originally, the tram stops contained advertising billboards, but because they were repeatedly covered with slogans, the tram company chose to remove the advertisements altogether. Each tram station became a vast white canvas for broadcasting political demands and reflections on the state of the protests. For instance, a protester made her way to the roof of a tram station on December 8, 2019 (marking the sixth month of the movement), to spray "From the beginning of summer…to the heart of a biting winter."

The graffiti was significant on two levels. First, it represented the persistence and continuing vitality of the movement for those engaged in it. It was crucial that the message "no relenting or conceding" be spread, "until the demands of the movement are met." To maintain this level of motivation and momentum in a social movement is extraordinarily difficult, calling for one mobilization after another, so whenever temporal milestones were met, they were celebrated with great fervor, reminding people that the struggle and enthusiasm continue despite immense odds. Second, spaces and materials of every medium and variety effectively became resources at the disposal of the struggle; everything was appropriated and made "useful," sometimes in spontaneous and improvisational ways, sometimes in carefully orchestrated ones.

following: Police fired tear gas to disperse protesters gathering around the Central Government Office in Hong Kong, China, June 12, 2019. Despite the march has been given a letter of no objection, the police decides to disperse the peaceful crowds.

These practices situate the struggle at the heart of urban life, posing questions about how the public might imagine a life together in the metropolis, and how the city might be transformed. These two points can effectively be collapsed: considering how this struggle persisted without any determined end in sight, the vitality of the movement can be found in the ways that the protesters "made use of the city," in the imbrication between the struggle and everyday life.

The appropriation of space and things in the urban environment is compelled by circumstance.

Kong

Sampson Wong and Merve Bedir Hong

Kong

For example, erecting roadblocks with the use of road signs and various sorts of detritus establishes a form of delay, a material block of spatialized time that allows protesters to establish distance from the approaching police and affords them a means to escape. To inhabit and make use of a space together amplifies a shared sense of power, whether physical or symbolic in nature. At the same time, different roles can be observed, allowing each person within the space to participate in, share, and enact that power in different ways. Being alert to the spaces that we find ourselves in and testing the concrete uses and possibilities that they afford by using them together, supports the vitality and the sustainability of the movement.

A thriving accelerated capitalist metropolis exists in Hong Kong. But it is also a metropolis in which the protests have created a frantic and elusive "present": the city is in perpetual flux, in a state of continuous unrest, political contestation, and antagonistic dispute about the uses of the city, which has never assumed a definitive or consolidated form. What takes place is an "unsettled urbanism," that goes against a deterministic understanding of space, where people's continuous movement creates the urban space.

FROM CONCRETE DEMANDS TO
ABSTRACT DESIRES
There has been no consensus about the name of the 2019 Hong Kong protests. The lack of a name agreed to by all in part reflects the dynamic and diverse political demands that have emerged and developed. First it was named the Anti-Extradition Law Amendment Bill Movement (Anti-ELAB Movement) because the protests were initially triggered by the very concrete demand for withdrawing an amendment to the extradition bill, which would allow Hongkongers to be extradited to China. After the bill was formally withdrawn, others named the protests variously to capture other political desires that consolidated following the first month of the protests: Hong Kong's democracy movement, the anti-authoritarian

Sampson Wong and Merve Bedir

movement, the summer of dissent, the "revolution of our times," the be water revolution, or the water revolution. Each of these names is no doubt an attempt to capture the central spirit or the modality of the protests.

The protests quickly moved beyond the issue of the extradition bill. The participants in the movement gradually shifted their focus to police brutality, arrest of activists, the government's unjust handling of the extradition bill, and more longstanding demands for democratization. The protest then became discursively flexible enough to sustain itself by, on the one hand, absorbing a range of political desires, and on the other, overcoming the potential split in the movement when some political demands were met by authorities. The movement benefited from the abstract goals of "Free Hong Kong" and "Fight for Freedom, Stand with Hong Kong," which became a broad banner uniting the participants, but also served as an "impossible" goal that boosted the protest actions to continue. Participants in the movement began to think that the goal was to "liberate" every aspect of the city; only a truly transformed Hong Kong would signal an end to the movement. This thus created room and the urge for deliberations to preempt the potential retreat of the movement. The movement's abstract also served the function of enabling citizens to participate in a movement that did not explicitly call for an institutional arrangement for the city.

following: Bouquets of white flowers pile up outside a shopping mall where a youth plunged to his death protesting against the proposed extradition bill. Hundreds of thousands of people rally and walk pass the mall earlier on that day. There are "almost 2 million people" joining the march according to the organizers, in Hong Kong, China, June 17, 2019.

Protesters take to the streets holding lights for Hong Kong's annual pro-democracy march which organizers estimated that 550,000 people have participated in Hong Kong, China, July 1, 2019. Picture taken with a long exposure.

UNSETTLED URBANISM

The unprecedented spatial expansion of the protests across the city, encompassing all types of spaces, was complemented by a temporal stretch: a week of struggle formally began on weekend afternoons, but the breadth of the struggle stretched into

Sampson Wong and Merve Bedir Hong

Kong

80

Sampson Wong and Merve Bedir

Kong

the workday with the strikes, and into the mornings and evenings, until it became coextensive with time itself; quotidian life and the struggle became virtually one and the same thing. This spatiotemporal stretch lead to the continuous production of new ideas, concepts, and forms of intervention—a sense of novelty in the experimentation of living that can overcome the grueling fatigue that one encounters in social movements situated in more conventional, designated sites of representation and struggle.

Unsettled Urbanism examines this experimental use of urban space from within, i.e., the relationship between the movement and the urban environment. Of course, such a discussion also requires looking at the ways in which the state makes use of urban space in strategic response to the movement's appropriation of the city, enforcing certain uses of the city while excluding and illegalizing others.

One of the most important aspects of the protests is that occupation of certain urban sites was not the priority; conveying the message through decentralization and mobility, i.e., the blink-of-an-eye speed and effectiveness of the people on the street, was paramount. Cloud-based, open-source instant messaging and forum applications facilitated a coalescence of the physical and digital space, expanding the movement and public space to a third space. As such, the city was transformed to a space of extreme interaction and moving together, an open and decentralized system that is young, fluid, and formless.

Unsettled Urbanism identifies three points about the spatial character of the Hong Kong protests (June 2019–January 2020): *Be Water*, focuses on the movement of people defining the city and the spatial condition; *Transformed Typologies* focuses on the spaces and typologies that have been completely transformed through alternate usage, such as shopping malls, metros, airports, schools, police stations, homes, pedestrian bridges, streets, and hills; and *Technology as Affordance*, focuses on the use of smart phones, communication and forum applications, and subverting surveillance technologies.

Sampson Wong and Merve Bedir

BE WATER

In the early stages of the Hong Kong protests, water imaginary was employed to denote a very particular behavior of the participants: in order to evade police surveillance and arrests, the crowd retreated once they were confronted by the police, and regrouped and reemerged quickly to initiate another street action. In part, the "Be water" motto reflects what people learned from the Occupy protest in 2014, which was framed as a form of failed activism particularly because of its static and "solid" nature and protesters' choice not to retreat when they were confronted the police. In online discussions, military terms were employed to discuss and discredit the effectiveness of occupying; it was suggested that "positional warfare" (occupying) should be completely abandoned, and "mobile warfare" should be championed.

Thus, from the outset, in naming the movement "Water Revolution," the protesters were calling for intensive and recurring protest events to be continuously played out without limiting them to a specific time or space. The networked nature of the movement, its decentralized and distributed mobilization and "leaderless" organization, were connected to this liquid imaginary: multifaceted forms of actions and events were incessantly organized and realized in the city to avoid the movement from fixating on one particular form of action. As such, the water imaginary concerns the ebbs and flows of varying types of actions, how they come and go quickly. As the motto "Be water" and the call for a "Water Revolution" were embraced, diverse forms of actions were imagined to be most effective for sustaining the movement in the long run, since a single, monolithic form would eventually be suppressed.

The forms, or rather formlessness, of these performances is crucial: protesters made use of many types of urban spaces and gradually spread

following: Riot police march on the street and fire tear gas to disperse protesters gathered in an area where the Chinese government's liaison office is located in Hong Kong, China, July 21, 2019.

Riot police wrestle protesters down and beat them with batons as the officers chasing them down the street in a shopping district in Hong Kong, China, August 11, 2019.

Black-Clad protesters, defying a police ban on protest marches, have surrounded a police station and occupied a main traffic junction in Hong Kong, China, August 11, 2019.

Kong

Sampson Wong and Merve Bedir Hong

Kong

85

Sampson Wong and Merve Bedir Hong

Kong

Sampson Wong and Merve Bedir

Hong

Kong

their varying actions geographically to almost all parts of the city. It is the process of experimentation with forms of actions and how they flow through the cityscape that connects to the imaginary of water most deeply.

TRANSFORMED TYPOLOGIES

During the protests, *shopping malls* were first used as refuge from the police but also from the heat and humidity outside. In time, shopping mall atriums became spaces of representation, with hanging banners related to the movement and its five demands. The protest anthem was sung and forums were organized in the atriums. These uses transformed the shopping mall from a space of capitalist consumption to a space of insurgency, the mall's vertical atrium space replacing the city square or the legislative council. In addition, *shops* became places of collectivity, hubs for supplies for protest actions, as well as pit stops to share stories and tactics.

During the first half of August 2019, *Hong Kong International Airport* and the roads to it were occupied for days, transforming the very airport from a space of transition and nonbelonging to a space of gathering and resistance. The arrivals hall was a place to greet friends and address the global community. Protesters chose to speak in person with those visiting Hong Kong about the reality of what was happening in the city.

The streets of action were not the pedestrian "high streets," but often the roads planned for automobiles. Protesters attempted to return these spaces to pedestrians through several means. Metal barriers by the roads, which are normally used to control circulation along the pedestrian walkways, were dismantled for a more efficient movement of people. These were used to stop the flow of cars and police vehicles, transforming the asphalt into a pedestrian street, as well as a canvas for people to

Jennifer Yip and Merve Bedir, The airport as an infrastructure became a site of gathering and communication instead of its actual function of transition and temporariness, 2019.

following: Crowds of protesters march from Hong Kong international airport to a nearby suburb town after they have tried to "stress test" airport transportation routes and suspend airline service in Hong Kong, China, September 1, 2019.

Sampson Wong and Merve Bedir

Hong

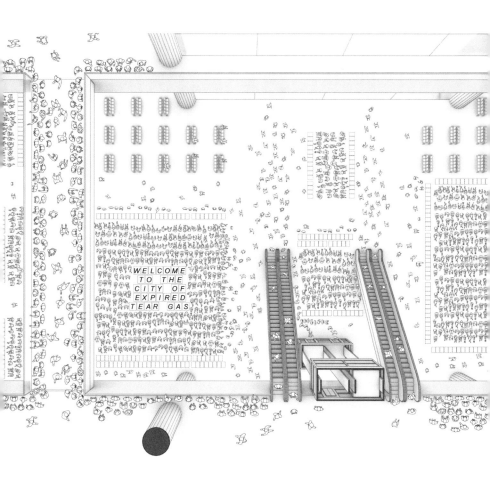

WELCOME
TO THE
CITY OF
EXPIRED
TEAR GAS

Kong

Sampson Wong and Merve Bedir Hong

Kong

express their thoughts for all to see. A call for strike resulted in the Central Business District streets being completely blocked to automobiles by distributing objects—bricks, bamboo sticks, and so forth—as obstacles. *Pedestrian bridges*, previously functional spaces of linkage that allow pedestrian movement to run smoothly and not disturb larger infrastructural automobile arteries, were transformed into places to share, display, and engage with fellow community members. The Lennon walls along the pedestrian bridges have become spaces of and by the people—spaces for sharing demands, desires, protest calendars, information boards, and so on.

Urban nature itself has been part of the movement. Perhaps the most common of all things within the city, Lion Rock is a significant part of Hong Kong's cultural landscape and collective identity; it was utilized for a human chain several times throughout the movement, actively reflecting the meaning of belonging back to the city and the urban space. The choice of Lion Rock displays a continuation of the people's movement in representation.

Hong Kong homes are known to be small and made for households small in size. Therefore, they are inevitably the most private part of the city. During the movement, however, they were transformed from individual, private spaces to mobile and public ones. Individual homes, linked via smart phones, became the distributed nodes of organization, where ideas of protest were generated by individuals or groups of friends, shared, discussed, and evaluated, only to then be leveraged by more people.

In this constellation, places of institutional power became nothing but stage sets. Spaces such as the police station or the legislative council were revealed to not be responsive during the protests. Police stations were literally made into fortresses by the police with nets set up along their entire facades and large barricades at street level diverting pedestrian movement to the opposite side of the street. The legislative council was similarly closed and fortified from July 2019—when the protesters occupied the council—until October 2019.

TECHNOLOGY AS AFFORDANCE

Technology has been an affordance to the movement on three levels: first, it was used in direct interventions on the street such as extinguishing tear-gas canisters and avoiding surveillance; second, technology facilitated the way people organized and mobilized; and third, the use of digital space fundamentally transformed the experience and perception of the city and urban space.

Protesters avoided surveillance by covering the CCTV cameras on the street or taking them down. Once knowledge of how to do this was discovered, like other interventions, it was quickly learned, communicated, and iterated elsewhere on the street at the protesters' own initiative. On October 4, 2019, the rarely used colonial-era Emergency Regulations Ordinance was invoked to implement the Prohibition on Face Covering Regulation (PFCR), i.e., the anti-mask law banning protesters from covering their faces during protests. People painted their faces, wore masks depicting political figures, but also made digital projections of other anonymous faces on their own face and created glare with mobile phone light held against the police to resist the anti-mask law and surveillance. Tracking systems (both CCTVs and ticketing) in the city's underground transport led to people abandoning this infrastructure, while it became a space of violence, and was gradually weaponized, physically and digitally, starting in June 2019.

Secondly, the self-organization and mobilization of protesters using open-source mobile communication applications and platforms showed the possibilities that the digital space can afford in relation to the body and urban space. LIHKG and Telegram were the two most important digital applications during the protests. Individually or in groups of friends, people shared ideas about

following: Protesters hurl Molotov cocktails to riot police on the campus of the Chinese University of Hong Kong, China, November 5, 2019. The clash unfolds at a barricaded bridge leading to the campus. Police officers fire hundreds of rounds of tear gas and rubber bullets and students throwback Molotov cocktails, bricks and firing bows with arrows.

Riot police fire water cannon to disperse protesters outside the Hong Kong Polytechnic University, China, November 17, 2019. The clash begins as police move in to clear the occupied campus and the protesters respond with bricks and petrol bombs.

Sampson Wong and Merve Bedir

Hong

Kong

Sampson Wong and Merve Bedir

Hong

Kong

different forms of action in the online forum LIHKG, and then on Telegram; they were then able to organize around the actions they were in favor of, to substantiate them. These processes involved anonymous participants, and gradually led to a de facto crowdsourcing of ideas on the possible types of protest actions. From June 2019 to January 2020, novel and creative protest acts (both violent and nonviolent) were realized in turn, and those that were not favored were naturally eliminated, sustaining creative energy throughout. As such, two problems were avoided: First, the participants would not repeat a specific type of action for a long period of time and when one type of action was deemed ineffective, it would be reduced. Secondly, the short attention span of the public and the media would not be an obstacle for the movement, as they are continuously fed with new "performances." This way, the movement embraced a horizontal and open mode of organization and mobilization, leading to an efficiency and acceleration of the movement, which was afforded by the digital platforms and their temporality. This model made it possible to avoid activists and leaders with hierarchical roles and single-line, centralized decision-making mechanisms within the movement.

Ultimately, the city and urban space were experienced fundamentally differently by those in the movement. The ideas and actions that people favored and substantiated were also continuously elaborated on site by actively using social media and mobile applications. These were used as real-time learning and self-organizing tools to develop tactics of mobility and protection, move between different parts of the city, avoid and extinguish tear-gas on location, avoid surveillance and police spots, navigate streets and barricades, transition between the lines of protest, locate first aid and supply stations, and inform those who didn't want to be involved in the protests about hotspots. This kind of utilization led to overlapping memories of digital and physical spaces, streamlining them to enable a new experience and production of urban space that is neither solely digital nor physical (bodily), but a coalescence of both.

Sampson Wong and Merve Bedir

EPILOGUE

This essay has articulated the nature of urban insurgency in Hong Kong, highlighting how protest action flows through urban space, and how it unsettles, reimagines, and transforms each space. It also reflects on how social movements in the last decade manifest as "urban political movements," and turn "the urban" itself into a resource for rebellion blocking the accelerated capitalist city. This both documents and calls for an understanding of how collective spatial intelligence is created, how the city is relived, and how the city and the public entered a continuous state of becoming during Hong Kong protests, but also elsewhere around the world. As people take action, moving towards a reality without really knowing what it may be but knowing that the existing possibilities are not enough, it is a critical time to look at the city again.

PROJECT CREDITS

Merve Bedir and Sampson Wong with chongsuen, Monique Wong, Nicole Lau, Jennifer Yip

Hong Kong University, Add Oil Collective

The first iteration of Unsettled Urbanism was produced for the Twelve Cautionary Urban Tales *exhibition in Matadero, Madrid, with generous facilitation by the exhibition's curator Ethel Baraona Pohl*

Unsettled Urbanism is a research project about the possibilities for non-static, spatial coexistence during the first phase of the Hong Kong protests (June 2019–January 2020). Spatial design is assumed to be intended for permanence for the crowds, and therefore, it is inevitably controlling. These interpretations of public space show how flexibility, fluidity, and openness can define the possibility of another urbanism. Thus, this work is also an open question to the manner in which we presume spatial design should be implemented and lived. "All free men, wherever they may love, are citizens of Berlin" was a proclamation made at the peak of the Cold War in 1963 in front of the Berlin Wall, the wall being the emblem of a form of "divided urbanism." In 2019, a chorus of people across the globe echoed the phrase "I am a Hongkonger" in solidarity with the movement. While Hong Kong serves as "inspiration," it takes inspiration from internationalist solidarity, from cities elsewhere, contemporaries and friends, those struggle alongside them through urbanism.

Becoming Urban: Trajectories of Urbanization in Contemporary India

Sourav Kumar Biswas
and Rahul Mehrotra

Ir

India is at the cusp of a significant economic transition as its urban population is projected to exceed the rural by 2050. More than half of the world's population already live in cities. The global development discourse celebrates the role of growing cities in Africa and Asia that will house rural migrants while lifting them out of poverty. This narrative greatly simplifies the diversity of urbanization trajectories unfolding in the Global South. India's urbanization in particular, will be shaped by the proximity of cities to a densely populated hinterland that we call the *urban-agrarian field*. The megacities of Delhi, Mumbai, and 50 other million-plus agglomerations grow within a densely populated agrarian territory of rural hamlets, large villages and small-medium towns where people, goods, and capital flow via strong urban-rural linkages and circular migration. Millions of informal workers, migrants, and farmers who contribute to building up the urban economy have not benefited proportionally and remain invisible to urban development policy.

We believe that India's strict definition of the "urban" has excluded thousands of densely populated settlements from this characterization. This in turn has created an urban policy of blind spots towards non-urban places transforming under urbanization and migrants who straddle the urban-rural continuum. A limited imaginary of what cities should look like based on colonial and modernist lenses further excludes prolific settlement typologies that house the urban and rural poor from planning support. Within India's megacities, the dearth of institutional systems for aspirational rural migrants has contributed to splintering urbanism in the form of growing informal settlements or urban villages. The continued neglect of this territorial dynamic led to the catastrophic exodus of migrant workers from urban areas during the COVID-19 lockdown.

As cities grow beyond their boundaries and market forces expand into the unrecognized urban-agrarian field, the emergence of hybrid urban-rural settlements and novel agrarian-industrial livelihoods pose intriguing challenges for designers and planners. The question of how we live together in India's contemporary and future cities will require a territorial view and an anticipatory framework that productively engages with emergent conditions in the urban-agrarian field.

WHAT IS URBAN?

India has more than 640,000 settlements out of which only 7,935 are considered "towns." Maps that represent India's urbanization often highlight the million-plus cities as nodes with a visually outsized circle representing their massive population. However, these 53 million-plus agglomerations in India are home to only 13% of the total population. Restricting the study of urbanization to large cities ignores the unfolding market forces and other transformations taking place in the densely populated field of villages and small-medium towns. India's urban development policy and planning approach is not set up to address the relationship of metropolitan areas with small-medium towns and settlements not yet considered urban. This is largely due to the way the agrarian territory has been represented and the way the "urban" is defined.

The last Census from 2011 considers 31% of India's population as "urban." This statistic is derived from the assumption that the extents of an urban area can be clearly delineated within distinct spatial units, and that only the inhabitants within this unit can be characterized as "urban." Therefore, India's urban population refers to 377 million people who have been officially identified as residents of a "town." The urban population refers to people living within administrative units that considered Statutory or Census Towns by the government. Statutory Towns are settlements that have been assigned an urban local body by the State. Census Towns are settlements that meet three demographic criteria: population number, density, and economic activity.

The "rural" is defined as any area outside the boundaries of towns. The "rural" is simply a residual space that emerges from a statistical claim based on the construction of demographic thresholds. In India this metric-based differentiation between the urban and rural has left governance structures

Sourav Kumar Biswas and Rahul Mehrotra

In

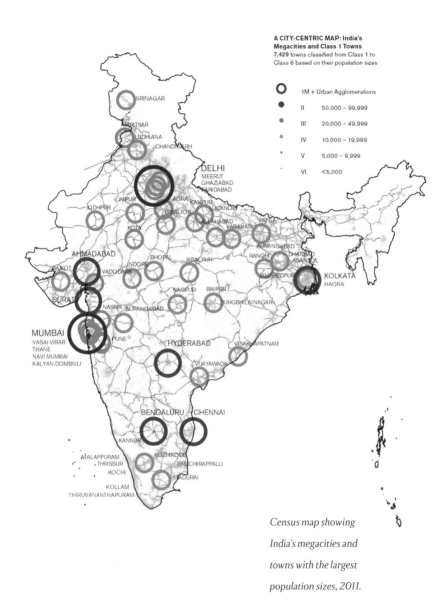

A CITY-CENTRIC MAP: India's Megacities and Class 1 Towns
7,429 towns classified from Class 1 to Class 6 based on their population sizes

◯		1M + Urban Agglomerations
●	II	50,000 – 99,999
●	III	20,000 – 49,999
·	IV	10,000 – 19,999
·	V	5,000 – 9,999
·	VI	<5,000

SRINAGAR

AMRITSAR
LUDHIANA
CHANDIGARH

DELHI
MEERUT
GHAZIABAD
FARIDABAD

JAIPUR   AGRA   KANPUR
JODHPUR   GWALIOR LUCKNOW
           KOTA   ALLAHABAD VARANASI PATNA

AHMADABAD   BHOPAL   JABALPUR   AURANGABAD
RAJKOT   RANCHI DHANBAD
      VADODARA   JAMSHEDPUR ASANSOL KOLKATA
SURAT   NAGPUR   RAIPUR   HAORA
      NASHIK AURANGABAD   DURGBHILAINAGAR

MUMBAI   PUNE
VASAI-VIRAR
THANE   HYDERABAD   VISAKHAPATNAM
NAVI MUMBAI
KALYAN-DOMBIVLI   VIJAYAWADA

       BENGALURU   CHENNAI
       KANNUR

MALAPPURAM   KOZHIKODE
  THRISSUR   TIRUCHIRAPPALLI
KOCHI
      KOLLAM   MADURAI
THIRUVANANTHAPURAM

Census map showing India's megacities and towns with the largest population sizes, 2011.

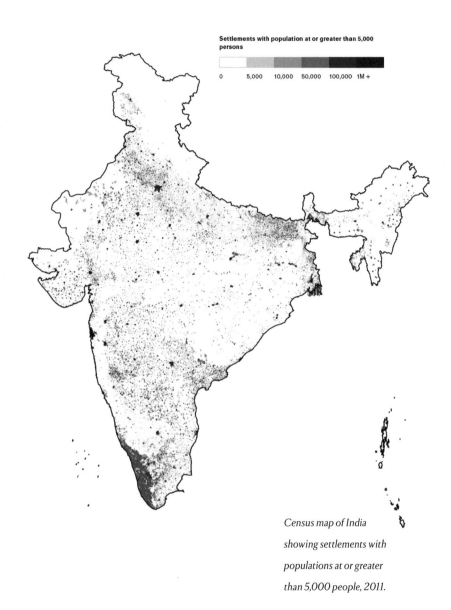

Settlements with population at or greater than 5,000 persons

0   5,000   10,000   50,000   100,000   1M +

Census map of India showing settlements with populations at or greater than 5,000 people, 2011.

Sourav Kumar Biswas and Rahul Mehrotra

In

unprepared to deal with the challenges of migration and informality. In order to approach India's urbanization challenges, we must first clarify the existing conceptual framework for the "urban." The Census of India uses three-fold demographic criteria to define the "urban." A critical examination of these statistical thresholds gradually unravel the limits of metric-based classification by considering settlements that meet only one Census criteria at a time.

Census Criteria One:
A Minimum Population of Five Thousand.
An essential condition of urbanity is to be found in the number of people that can support an economic base and create the demand for a range of facilities. The benefits of agglomeration begin with the idea that the larger the settlement, the greater the diversity of skillsets, ideas, and opportunities. In 1971, the Census of India set the minimum population number of five thousand as one of three criteria for urban areas. Today, more than thirty thousand settlements meet the population number criteria set by the Census. If India used this threshold as the sole criteria, the country would be 47% "urban."[1] However, there is no definitive argument for whether five thousand is an appropriate cutoff for India. If India adopted Mexico's criteria for urban, which is a minimum population of 2,500, India would be 66% urban. A mapping of settlements that meet these criteria of population size in India demonstrates the geographic spread of highly populated settlements—only a fraction of which are considered "urban."

1   See Arindam Jana and Teja Malladi, *Urban India 2015: Evidence* (Bengalore: Indian Institute of Human Settlements, 2015) and Aromar Revi et. al., *Urban India 2011: Evidence* (Bengalore: Indian Institute for Human Settlements, 2011).

Census Criteria Two: A Minimum Population Density of Four Hundred Persons Per Square Kilometer.
The concentration of people within a settlement is another indicator of urbanity. A high population density makes shared resources viable, subsidizes common services, and intensifies economic and social interactions. Density fosters opportunities. Urbanization has been celebrated

by economists and policy-makers as a process that leverages effects of networks and economies of scale arising from agglomeration. However, only nine countries in the world use population density as a criterion to define the urban. India uses a population density threshold of four hundred persons per square kilometer as the second criteria. By global standards, this threshold can be considered to be very high and thus quite restrictive. Germany considers any settlements with more than 150 persons per square kilometer as "urban." The cut-off of four hundred persons comes close to metropolitan densities of large but sprawling urban regions like those surrounding Boston, Houston, or Atlanta. Even so, if India used this threshold of density as the sole criteria, it would be 70% "urban."[2] A visualization of all settlements that meet the density criteria reveals a territory that spans the historically entrenched agrarian territory comprising hundreds of settlements along the Gangetic plain and other river systems. India's cities—with densities typically in the thousands—dot a territory that is itself quite dense. However, the incorporation of the third census criteria, which uses the metric of employment, eliminates almost all these settlements from the lens of urban policy and development. In fact, this is what dissuades urban and rural development policy-makers from pursuing strategies that could leverage the networked synergies of a densely populated territory.

Census Criteria Three: At least 75% of the Male Working Population Is Engaged in Non-Agricultural Pursuits.
The nature of socioeconomic processes within "urban" settlements—especially the heterogeneity of opportunities and the specialization of labor—is markedly different from "rural" settlements that are largely dependent on agriculture. While a population size determinant and cutoff for what is urban was introduced by the Census since 1881, the evaluation of whether a settlement has an "urban character" had historically been left to the discretion of the governing authorities. It was only through the formalization of an economic activity criteria in the Census of 1961 that this third criteria was introduced to quantitatively measure the dependence of a settlement to

2   Jana and Malladi, *Urban India 2015*, 24, and Revi, *Urban Indian 2011*, 12.

Sourav Kumar Biswas and Rahul Mehrotra

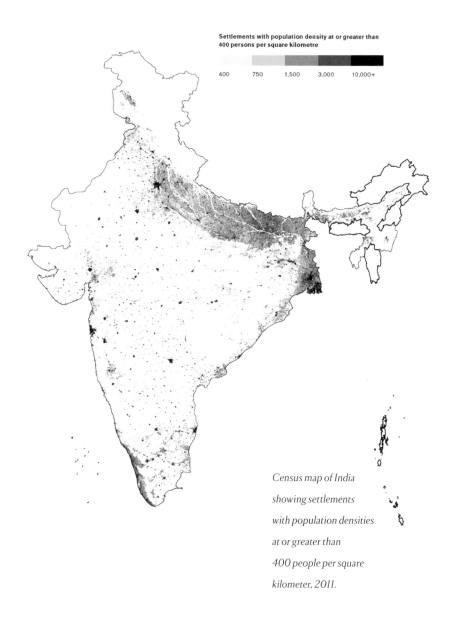

Settlements with population density at or greater than 400 persons per square kilometre

400   750   1,500   3,000   10,000+

Census map of India
showing settlements
with population densities
at or greater than
400 people per square
kilometer, 2011.

dia

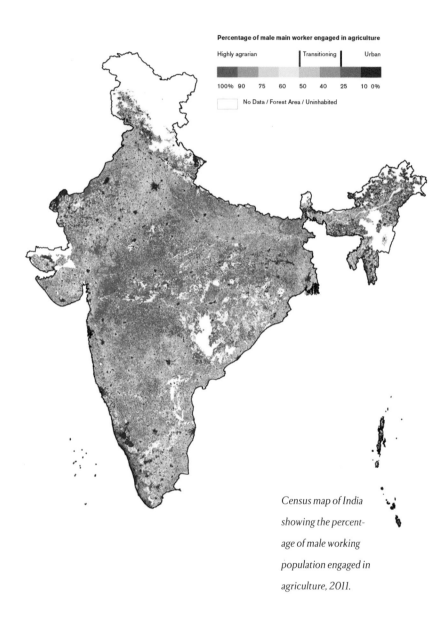

Percentage of male main worker engaged in agriculture

Highly agrarian | Transitioning | Urban

100% 90 75 60 50 40 25 10 0%

No Data / Forest Area / Uninhabited

Census map of India
showing the percent-
age of male working
population engaged in
agriculture, 2011.

Sourav Kumar Biswas and Rahul Mehrotra

Ir

agriculture and conversely to non-agricultural employment. As per the economic activity criteria, only a settlement where at least 75% of the male main working population is engaged in non-agricultural work can be considered "urban." Using this criterion alone, India would be only 36% "urban."[3] This is the only criterion that brings India's urban population significantly below 50%. Thus, India's urban-rural dichotomy is essentially determined by the measurement of "agrarian" and "non-agrarian" livelihoods. A criterion that is increasingly hard to determine or map, especially within rural areas where livelihoods are fluid and temporal in nature.

MAPPING INDIA'S HINTERLAND IN FLUX

India's "rural" territory is a statistical by-product of the Census. It is a residual category describing all places outside the boundaries of settlements considered "urban." However, the definitions and thresholds the Census uses to create this conceptual boundary depend upon a tenuous measurement of agricultural activity and related employment. To create the economic activity metric, the Census has to simplify the complex work profile of farmers who depend on non-agricultural income. The sociologist Dipankar Gupta points out that if you ask a villager his occupation, he will answer "farmer." But if you follow him through the day to see what he is doing at a particular time, he could be making bricks for construction, or heading to the labor market to find some temporary jobs in the town nearby.[4] Gupta found that even as people continue to live and work in villages, they are almost "urban" in terms of their work profile.

India's rural territory is dominated by a high-population density field of small-lot subsistence agriculture. After generations of inherited subdivisions, most of the landholdings in India are below five acres. As a result, the per capita income divide between urban and rural areas have expanded significantly. This divide drives the population of this agrarian hinterland to commute, temporarily migrate, or move to urban centers. The ubiquity of the railway network, other inexpensive transport

3   Jana and Malladi, 24, and Revi, 12.

4   Dipankar Gupta, "The Importance of Being 'Rurban': Tracking Changes in a Traditional Setting," *Economic & Political Weekly* 50, no. 24 (June 13, 2015): 38.

networks, and new forms of connectivity are only reinforcing historic patterns of migration from village to town as well as opening up new patterns of movement. New circuits of labor and capital are changing work profiles within villages as more non-agricultural opportunities become available in areas considered rural. Given this circulatory relationship, representations of the urban that highlight a set of (town) nodes which are neatly categorized into "urban" or "rural" is limiting. Rather, this territory is better conceptualized as an interconnected urban-agrarian field. India's urban-agrarian field is a human-dominated mosaic shaped by agrarian regimes where small-holder farmers engage with specific protocols and practices adapted to seasonal and ecological flows. The temporal nature of agrarian activity makes this territory a dynamic and restless source of goods and surplus labor. The sowing and harvesting seasons of rice and wheat—two of the most dominant crop-regimes in India— are limited to four months a year. This suggests that for up to six or eight months of a year, farmers are looking for other markets for their surplus products, finding other commodities to market, or simply finding non-agricultural jobs in larger villages or nearby towns to supplement their incomes.

If economic activity was measured in a dynamic way, India's rate of urbanization would fluctuate rather dramatically as many more livelihoods shift to non-agrarian jobs during lean agricultural seasons. It may be possible to project and visualize this dynamic labor shift away from agriculture at a territorial scale. Mapping the extents of specific crop regimes, such as rice, overlaid with the prevalence of marginal agrarian population offers a spatial proxy for which regions are more likely to shed surplus labor from farms to non-farm activities at a particular time of the year.

Urban and rural development policies are set up as dichotomous approaches to improving disparate places with distinct livelihoods. As such they are ill-equipped to address the needs of an increasingly mobile agrarian population. They do not respond to the dynamism inherent to India's urban-agrarian field. While the Census limits the conceptual

Census crop calendar for rice and labor cycles with maps showing rice-growing sub-districts, 2012, and the percentage of marginal agrarian workers in India (2011).

Sourav Kumar Biswas and Rahul Mehrotra

Ir

Crop Calendar for Rice and Labor Cycles

Autumn Rice (Kharid, Aus, Kar)

Jan	Feb	Mar	Apr	May	Jun	Jul	Aug	Sep	Oct	Nov	Dec

Sowing months   Harvesting months

Winter Rice (Rabi, Aman, Sali, Karthika)

Jan	Feb	Mar	Apr	May	Jun	Jul	Aug	Sep	Oct	Nov	Dec

Sowing months   Harvesting months

Rice growing sub-districts engage cultivators who are likely to hire additional agricultural laborers during the intensive months of harvesting and sowing periods

Rice growing sub-districts with high percentages of marginal agricultural workers are likely to release more surplus labor during lean agricultural months

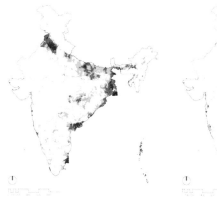

Rice-growing sub-districts (by water consumption)

0 m³ of water   954 m³

Map Data Source: Hoekstra, 2012 and MLInfoMap

Percentage of marginal agrarian workers in 2011
(including cultivators and agricultural laborers)

0   15   25   50   76

Map Data Source: Census of India 2011, MLInfoMap

framework with which to observe the realities of India's so-called hinterland, India's governance structures are set up to reinforce rather than overcome the very dichotomies that are being upended by aspirational households and transitioning settlements.

MEASURING AND MAPPING URBANIZATION

In the global imaginary, India is still a largely "rural" country because the official urbanization rate is derived from the government's metrics described in the preceding sections. India's use of a particularly narrow and restrictive economic activity criteria is the main reason why the country's urbanization rate is significantly below 50%. As economies within rural areas diversify, the reality is the farmer today can be more than a farmer and the census will fail to capture that given their methodological limitations.

In 2011, there were 116,430 villages where more than half the male workforce was non-agrarian.[5] The National Sample Survey Office findings on rural households from 2014 found that less than 60% of households considered rural were "agricultural"—defined as those having at least one member self-employed in farming, either in principal or subsidiary status, during the last 365 days. Even among "agricultural" households, over 40% of their income came from non-farming economic activities. Thus, an imperfect measure of economic activity has denied a vast number of highly populated settlements an "urban" administrative status and the support systems that come with it. Additionally, metrics that link people to places of residence rather than place of employment further contribute to a skewed image of how "urban" the population of the "rural" hinterland has become. The flows of labor and goods between India's agrarian settlements and large, medium, and small towns are unacknowledged—leaving urban planning unprepared for the flux inherent to the urban-agrarian field.

Since India's hinterland is a dynamic and restless source of goods, surplus labor, and an ecology dominated by human activity, the mapping of India's urbanization should represent

Sourav Kumar Biswas and Rahul Mehrotra

Ir

gradients of population densities and regimes of occupation across its territory. Economic prosperity from urbanization within capitalism manifests in various forms and are necessarily concentrated in a spatially and socio-economically uneven manner. The role of cities as historic sites of prosperity for villages has to be understood in terms of their spatial proximities to each other and to networks of transportation, communication, and utilities. How institutional investments can facilitate the connectivity between "agrarian" and "urban" economies to distribute prosperity more evenly, can only be understood by situating urbanizing settlements within a historically entrenched agricultural territory.

The mapping exercise as part of the *Becoming Urban* project for La Biennale di Venezia's 17th International Architecture Exhibition situates India's towns and cities within what could be referred to as the "agrarian field." The agrarian field is a densely populated territory with numerous settlements and agglomerations that have "urban" population characteristics but "rural" administrative structures and morphologies. The interaction of small-medium towns and metropolitan regions with this field is crucial to understanding the dynamics and corridors of migration. The agrarian field offers surplus labor which is highly connected to urban markets via extensive railway and highway networks. More than half of India's population live within one hour of a fifty thousand plus settlement.[6] Thus, settlements within this field are in constant flux—historically in the form of labor circuits and increasingly today in the form of capital flows.

The liberalization of India's economy in 1992 has unleashed market forces across this field. Industrialization in today's post-Fordist era is no longer constrained by centralized models that depend on a large city. In fact, it thrives upon decentralized logistics and big-box typologies that are more suited to geographies outside the city. The "urban-agrarian field" is a framework that allows us to examine the implications of these shifts since

5 Partha Mukhopadhyay, Marie-Hélène Zérah, Eric Denis, "Subaltern Urbanization Revisited," *India International Center Quarterly* 43, no. 3–4 (Winter 2016–Spring 2017): 26–41.

6 Hirotsugu Uchida and Andrew Nelson, "Agglomeration Index: Towards a New Measure of Urban Concentration," WIDER Working Paper, no. 2010/29 (Helsinki: United Nations University-World Institute for Development Economics Research, 2010), 14.

dia

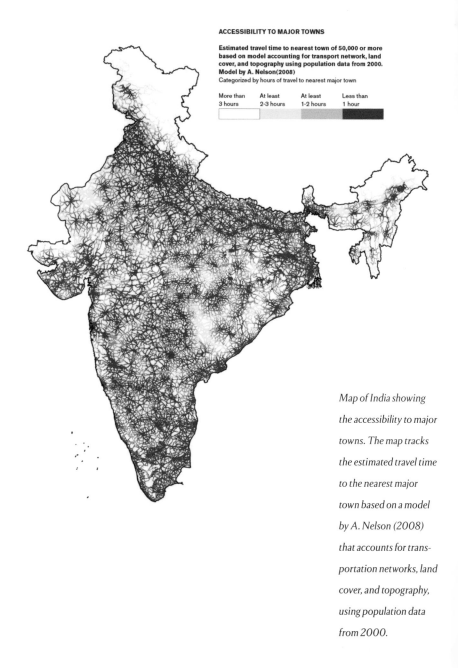

ACCESSIBILITY TO MAJOR TOWNS

Estimated travel time to nearest town of 50,000 or more based on model accounting for transport network, land cover, and topography using population data from 2000.
Model by A. Nelson(2008)
Categorized by hours of travel to nearest major town

More than 3 hours	At least 2-3 hours	At least 1-2 hours	Less than 1 hour

Map of India showing the accessibility to major towns. The map tracks the estimated travel time to the nearest major town based on a model by A. Nelson (2008) that accounts for transportation networks, land cover, and topography, using population data from 2000.

Sourav Kumar Biswas and Rahul Mehrotra

In

7   For a discussion of the "*desa-kota*" see Norton Ginsburg, "Extended Metropolitan Regions in Asia: A New Spatial Paradigm" and Terry McGee, "The Emergence of Desakota Regions in Asia: Expanding a Hypothesis" in *The Extended Metropolis: Settlement Transition in Asia*, eds. Norton Ginsburg, Bruce Koppel, Terry McGee (Honolulu: University of Hawaii, 1991), 27–46 and 47–67. For a discussion of the "rurban" see Aromar Revi, S. Prakash, Rahul Mehrotra, G. K. Bhat, Kapil Gupta, Rahul Gore, "Goa 2100: The Transition to a Sustainable RUrban Design," *Environment and Urbanization* 18, no. 1 (2006): 51–65; Pranav Sidhwani, "Farm to Non-Farm: Are India's Villages 'Rurbanizing'?" Working Paper (Deli, India: Centre for Policy Research, 2014), 1–29; and Gupta, "The Importance of Being 'Rurban': Tracking Changes in a Traditional Setting," 37–43.

8   Neil J. Brenner, "Theses on Urbanization," in *Implosions/Explosions: Towards a Study of Planetary Urbanization*, ed. Neil J. Brenner (Berlin: Jovis, 2014), 182.

the resulting economies, settlements, and ecologies do not neatly fit within categories like "urban" or "rural." The framework seeks to update the "*desakota*" and "rurban" concept for post-liberalization India where post-Fordist industrialization and neo-liberal planning paradigms are creating new circuits for labor and capital.[7]

By liberating our understanding of the urban from the fixation on the city, we could pave the way for the formulation of urban policy frameworks and planning paradigms that are prepared to face the novel challenges that emerge from the extended processes of urbanization in India and other geographies that face similar conditions of transition. In order to make this shift, urbanization has to be understood and mapped as a process involving varying degrees of concentrated land-use, increased connectivity, and fluid exchanges of capital, labor, and commodities within the urban-agrarian field and necessarily beyond the city.[8]

EMERGING PATTERNS OF URBANIZATION

India is essentially witnessing three key paradigm shifts in its pattern of urbanization. The first is the clear economic transition of large villages within the urban-agrarian field. These are rural settlements far removed from large-medium urban centers that are finding diverse ways to shift towards non-agrarian economies. Secondly, rapidly growing small-medium towns are witnessing much higher growth rates than large cities but building upon a fundamentally different organic settlement structure and form. Lastly, peri-urban transformations throughout India have been brought upon by the dramatic expansion of the built-up areas of large cities into agrarian landscapes and settlements driven by industrial decentralization and market-driven growth. The combination of these three shifts is transforming the landscape of India in fundamental ways that challenge our business as usual reading of urbanization in India.

Interestingly, none of these conditions result in the formation of entirely new settlements. Rather, existing settlements are expanding or urbanizing in situ. For the "rural" urbanizing settlements, either the city comes to them physically, or the economy of the "city" finds its way to settlements far removed from existing urban centers. Planned green field development by the state does not seem to compete with the rapid rate at which existing settlements are urbanizing in situ. Market-driven growth also fails to develop housing products at the price-point that India's migrants and transitioning households can afford. Therefore, the majority of India's future "urban" population will not be housed in top-down masterplans drawn up by the state or developers. Rather, settlements with distinctly "rural" morphologies or unplanned hybrid assemblages will become sites of economic opportunity for most of the households in the urban-agrarian field.

In order to respond to these shifts, planning frameworks and development policy have to necessarily be decentered from the static imaginary of the "city." Urban policy has to adapt to processes such as internal migration and informal employment without privileging the "urban" over the "rural" or the "formal" over the "informal." The process of urbanization in India is socioeconomically manifested in the rise of the informal economy, and spatially manifested by self-built forms of city-making. Thus far, informality has become the dominant mode of production of space within towns and villages across the urban-agrarian field. An anticipatory and adaptive approach to planning and infrastructural deployment is critical to providing amenities to such organic growth. Much like the informal settlements within India's metropolitan cities, the transitions taking place outside large cities have barely been mapped and have not had development plans or planning regulations directing their growth.

In such a context, the same frameworks that failed to equip large cities with the capacity to manage informal growth cannot

Sourav Kumar Biswas and Rahul Mehrotra

Ir

succeed in supporting transitions within small-medium towns and large villages. Funding models and policy mechanisms that cater to transitioning settlements depend upon identifying shifts in livelihood and then supporting the economic opportunities that are emerging spontaneously within the urban-agrarian field. To facilitate this approach, the dynamics of urbanization that are taking place outside the jurisdiction of large-medium urban centers have to be first mapped and studied at both site-specific and territorial scales in order to anticipate and prepare for future emergent patterns.

In summary, urban planning in India has to adapt to two major realities that define the trajectories of urbanization today. Firstly, settlements are more connected to each other than ever before, creating a greater reach for urbanization and market forces to impact livelihoods. Due to the development of para-transit modes, expansion of the highway network, and the ubiquitous presence of the railway network, distant commuters and short-term migrants can access the "urban" economy of large-to-small towns without permanently leaving their villages.

Secondly, settlements beyond large cities are becoming sites of opportunity in and of themselves. The evolution of industrial paradigms that thrive on decentralized production units and extended logistical networks allows global corporations as well as individuals to set up their enterprises in places far removed from large cities. While access to cities as markets is still desirable, it is no longer necessary or even pragmatic to situate production, processing, and distribution logistics within large cities. Near-universal access to mobile phones and innovations in banking have created more avenues for urbanization. The influx of remittances from cities within India and abroad are beginning to change many "rural" landscapes, as returning migrants or extra capital spurn local investments and businesses.

A city-centric understanding of the urbanization in India has obfuscated its linkages to this restless and dynamic agrarian field. The metrics of the Census and the government's development policies perpetuate an ideological urban-rural dichotomy that has become irreversibly fuzzy. How can urban policy and governance accommodate urbanizing settlements that are rendered invisible due to the methodological adherence to Census thresholds? Visualizing and contextualizing the territories of urbanizing economies is certainly the first step to preparing an anticipatory urban governance and development policy—one that understands the shifts within transitioning regions and supports the rise of economic opportunity in thousands of settlements within the urban-agrarian field.

The "Becoming Urban" installation at the Biennale uses multiple media to deconstruct the dichotomies of formal-informal, urban-rural, and ecology-politics at various scales. By taking a territorial view, the fluidity of the urban-agrarian field is registered through the movement of millions of seasonal migrants and commuters. An overview of transitioning settlements beyond India's metropolitan regions highlights the recurring juxtaposition of so-called formal-informal morphologies across the changing hinterland. At the sub-continental scale, the dichotomy of political versus ecological imaginaries such as the Indo-Gangetic Plain forces us to speculate on a reconceptualization of political borders. The Indo-Gangetic Plain is the most extensive, densely populated territory in the planet spanning two river basins encompasses 2.5 million square kilometer. The Indus and Ganga River basins are home to more than eight hundred million people who are divided by some of the strongest political borders between India, Pakistan, Bangladesh, Nepal, and Afghanistan. The contested borders dividing various political entities within a landscape unit defined by water is yet another ideological barrier that has to be reimagined to effectively address rapid urbanization and massive displacements in the era of climate change. For architects and designers to play a meaningful role in these precarious times requires us to acknowledge and empower the lived experiences of millions of households who traverse the imagined borders that are reinforced by planning and policy.

NASA Earth Observatory image showing a nighttime light visualization of India.

PROJECT CREDITS

Rahul Mehrotra and Sourav Kumar Biswas with Nondita Correa Mehrotra, Isabel Oyuela-Bonzani, Juan-Davide Grisales, Angela Sniezynski, Lamia Almuhanna, Maria Letizia Garzoli, and Dan Borelli

Harvard University Graduate School of Design, The Lakshmi Mittal and Family South Asia Institute, Architecture Foundation

Sourav Kumar Biswas and Rahul Mehrotra

Ir

NIGHT-TIME LIGHT VISUALIZATION OF INDIA

Urbanization is a spatial and temporal process that is not justifiably represented by static snapshots in time and discrete statistical thresholds perpetuated by the Census.

Datasets like the night-time lights offer a spatially-grounded view of the networks and intensities of urbanization. As a constantly monitored phenomena, if offers a time-based understanding of expansions and transformation. While this is a reliable proxy to observe territorial patterns, it cannot capture the kinds of socio-economic transformations that characterize India's transitioning agrarian settlements. The integration of the granular Census data along with spatial, time-based datasets like these can offer a more robust foundation for identifying the subtle and dramatic shifts within India's urban-agrarian field.

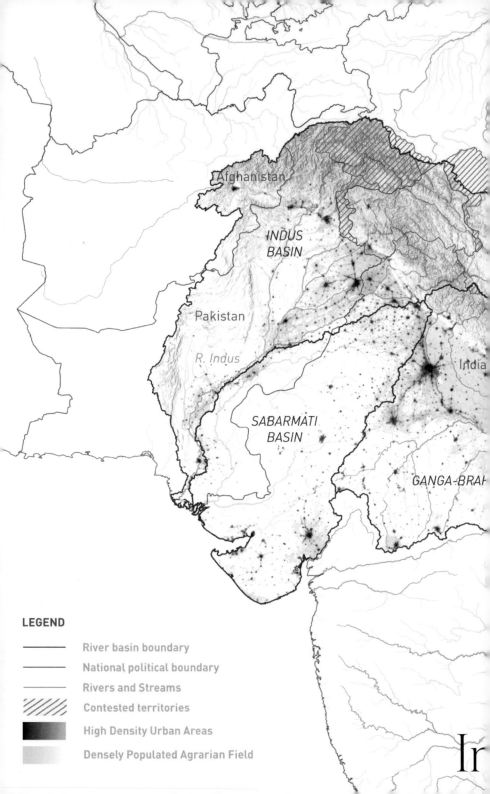

Afghanistan

INDUS
BASIN

Pakistan

R. Indus

India

*SABARMATI
BASIN*

GANGA-BRAH

LEGEND

————	River basin boundary
————	National political boundary
————	Rivers and Streams
/////	Contested territories
▰▰▰	High Density Urban Areas
▱▱▱	Densely Populated Agrarian Field

In

Map showing the trans-boundary urban-agrarian field in the Indo-Gangetic basins.

dia

With(in)

MIT Media Lab
City Science group

Mexico/

This is a story about connection. The MIT Media Lab City Science group presents an immersive view into the worlds of three women in three settlements: Eva in Guadalajara, Mexico; Gihan in Cairo, Egypt; and MamaG in Port Harcourt, Nigeria. Through visual storytelling and projection mapping onto domestic objects, we experience activities from the mundane to the surreal, from the deeply meaningful to the inconsequential. We visit the fringe neighborhoods and community centers of Guadalajara, the vertical slums and bustling streets of Cairo, and the tiny homes and crowded markets of Port Harcourt. In the lives of each individual, we examine the micro and the macro, from the gentle care of fixing one's hair each morning to the cultural swells of holidays, religious ceremonies, and funerals. In these places, far from our own, we learn and inquire, we gather and we listen, in the hope of better understanding the complexity of the world around us and new possibilities for how we will live together in the future.

As extreme urbanization unfolds at an astounding pace, all three locations reflect the chaos and the importance of community. One woman's journey can be both individual and global when viewed in the context of the others. We ask ourselves: how does rapid urbanization impact the community we seek, and how do intimate domestic activities such as food preparation and celebration reflect a larger cultural context?

EVA

It is December in Lomas del Centinela, a principality in Guadalajara, and Eva wakes up early to make her trek to the city. She is a mother of four, grandmother of three, skilled seamstress, and community leader. Eva wears bold clothes, often handmade and adorned, and has vibrant, blonde hair. Nicknamed "La Barbie del Centinela," she is easy to spot and recognize as she makes her way through the dusty streets. Lomas del Centinela is located high on a hill with beautiful views below, but the steep slope of the hill and the rough terrain make it difficult to reach, and the public transportation is poor.

MIT Media Lab
City Science group

Mexico/

Eva heads toward the center of town, past the crowded homes under constant construction—each one or two floors and filled with multiple generations of the same family. Rebar is left intentionally sticking out from the rooftops so that new floors and extensions can be added in the future. In the community, they are called *varillas de la esperanza*, or "bars of hope," that signal the potential of upward growth and new opportunities.

The children who live in Lomas also present an image of hope. They wander and play and take care of each other. Lomas is home to many single mothers, and during the day many women work in the wealthy houses of the nearby Zapopan neighborhood. A pine tree forest marks the separation between Zapopan and Lomas: swimming pools and golf courses on one side, and the tiny colorful homes of Lomas on the other. The inequality is stark and evident.

During the Christmas holiday, many people will rely on Eva to create a community that they might not otherwise have. Today, Eva is on her way to the center of Guadalajara to gather ingredients for the Posadas: *hojas, masa, carne, chiles y agua*. Eva's shopping trip is long and complicated. Her community is far from the center of the city and public transportation is unpredictable. She finally arrives at the *tianguis* market. During market days, streets are closed off to cars and space is opened up for endless, abundant fresh food stalls. It is the ultimate market and all of the food is local, with only the onions being imported.

Tonight, Eva hosts a Mexican party with traditional food cooked on a tiny electric stove. Her family is thrilled and eager when it is finally time to eat and they spend the evening eating and chatting. When the tamales are gone, the family heads to another house across the street to visit Eva's extended family. They drink tequila and listen to music until the late hours of the evening.

Eva stands by an electricity tower. Lomas del Centinela's wide sky is entangled with power cables—getting close enough one can hear the crackle and hiss of corona discharge. Lomas' inhabitants call it huachicol, meaning "sucking" water and electricity from the public grid, Guadalajara, Mexico, December 2019.

Tianguis on a Sunday afternoon. The tianguis *are street markets dating back to prehispanic times. They remain today as the main form of popular trade in Mexico. They are temporary and open different days of the week in different streets, Guadalajara, Mexico, December 2019.*

Egypt/Nigeria

GIHAN

Cairo is red. An ocean of brick buildings takes over the margins of the Nile from the north to the south. Millions of housing units are built illegally on former agricultural and desert land to house migrants from Upper Egypt and the Delta, a rapid and relentless process that the government is incapable of stopping. The concrete structures and brick walls are intentionally left unfinished, a common practice to avoid taxation and divert attention. Each building is five or more floors. These vertical slums also have rebar protruding from the top floors. Like in Lomas, they allow for future additions.

The sun is about to rise, and the first call to prayer echoes through the streets of Ezbet Khairallah. Gihan is home getting ready for the day. Her hair, dyed vibrant red like her city, is gently tucked into her hijab. She walks down the dark, winding, concrete staircase into the street and just across the road to her work. The Dawar Kitchen has become a home away from home for Gihan and for many other women in Ezbet Khairallah. The kitchen is her community, and it provides support and communion. There are nine women total who work in the kitchen. Some are Egyptian migrants and some are Syrian refugees. Their work has offered each of them a new life. For Gihan this fresh start means that her mark as a divorced woman has not held her back and that here, amongst these women, she is accepted. The kitchen is in constant motion as women shift nonstop around a large metallic table at the center of the kitchen. They work swiftly and confidently as they prepare the required meals, laughing, gossiping, and singing.

It's almost noon when a cell phone alarm sounds signaling the second call to prayer. Some women, though not all, make space in a corner of the kitchen and lay small colorful carpets facing the windows in the direction of Mecca. After the prayer, they set up the big table for lunch.

Gihan stares at the sky from the rooftop opening at the entrance to her home. She had just moved to Ezbet Khairallah with her three kids, with faith that she would find a new life and new beginnings, Cairo, Egypt, February 2020.

Gihan and her son leave home to go to the market downstairs. Cairene informal communities are vertical, growing up to 15 floors in some areas. Floor by floor, additions are made as the family grows and newcomers increase the demand for rental apartments, Cairo, Egypt, February 2020.

Mexico/

MIT Media Lab
City Science group

Mexico/

The Dawar Kitchen is a beautiful and warm place to spend time and eating together is the best part. Every inch of the table is covered with salads, warm dishes, and pita bread, all passed around and eaten with their hands. The meals are so beautifully plated that it is easy to wonder if this is some special occasion, but the women deflect this idea. "We like to spoil ourselves," they say.

In the afternoon Gihan stops by a stall at the food market downstairs to buy some oranges that she needs for dinner. The streets are vibrant in the evening: food vendors moving about in their carts, blinking LED street lights, small boys running around, elderly people at the coffee shops, and fire pits on the sidewalks to warm up.

We walk to Gihan's apartment—up and up and up the stairs, all five floors. She leaves her shoes outside the door and invites us in. Her walls are bright pink and her floors are thick with densely patterned carpets, contrasting with the monotonous bricks of the city outside. She warms up taro soup for her daughter and two sons. It is something that she prepared on her day off, making enough to feed them throughout the week. The family eats with their hands, while the spirals and finials of the carpet swirl out beneath them. From the balcony window the city hums and the last call to prayer begins.

MamaG illuminates the bedroom with her phone flashlight. Newly widowed, she travelled from Port Harcourt to her husband's ancestral village in order to bury him and honor him with a large traditional ceremony. As a sign of prestige, she's the only person who's assigned a room for herself for the event, Eket, Nigeria, January 2020.

A boy cleans a big water tank from inside as he was the only one small enough to enter. The tank will store water for more than 300 guests that will come for the funeral festivities, Eket, Nigeria, January 2020.

MAMAG

MamaG stands for Mother General. She is the mother of all at the Flyover Market in Port Harcourt, Nigeria, a strip of land above the train tracks and below the highway. Here, early in the morning, MamaG sets up her stall. MamaG, like many others, works every day of the week, and this petty trade supplies her entire income— a complex contrast to the wealthy who benefit from living in this rich oil capital.

Egypt/Nigeria

In the market you can buy food, CDs, and secondhand clothing, or visit a hairdresser, tailor, shoemaker, manicurist, or healer. In Port Harcourt, everything happens at the market. At her stall, MamaG doesn't stop for one second. Clients are constantly coming to buy drinks and bus tickets from her, or to trade or deposit money. In addition to her work making and selling potions, she also works as an informal banker and carefully accounts for all loans by hand in a small notebook.

By the end of the day MamaG closes her stall with the help of her son and gives fifty naira (0.23 USD) to night watchers to take care of her belongings. She used to share business responsibilities with her husband but now she needs to operate on her own, with her son stopping by at times. As we walk through the market, we see flyers pasted to pillars with the likeness of Harry Bassey, a.k.a. PapaG. The flyers share details of his upcoming funeral. Here in this crowded market teeming with life we are reminded that we are here to attend the funeral and help MamaG in any way we can. In Nigeria you are buried in your ancestral home, and so PapaG must be buried in Eket as his father and his father's father were. MamaG will need to pay fifty times more than the price of her rent on the funeral, but she will do so without a second thought as this is of utmost cultural importance.

When the day arrives, MamaG loads the trunk of a rented minibus with yams and her favorite spices. She is joined by her "sisters," close friends from her church. They spend two hours on the road to Eket, some time in travel and some time at the numerous police checkpoints on the way. When we arrive at the village, we are immediately struck by the contrast to Port Harcourt. The village is lush and green and the air is clear and fresh.

At the front of the family house, a small man is digging a grave for PapaG, while other village men drink hard liquor nearby. We hear soft rhythmic beats emanating from the back of the house. It's not music yet, it's the women pounding okazi leaves. In the next five days they will be cooking nonstop in an effort to feed all three hundred villagers and their guests. The only woman who won't cook is MamaG. According to tradition, the widow rests until the last day of rites.

MIT Media Lab
City Science group

Mexico/

In the following days we witness a rich celebration that, for untrained Western eyes, resembles more a wedding than a funeral. From the first rite when a goat is sacrificed and shared among the neighbors, until the last one, when MamaG's head is shaved, we are immersed in beauty and tradition. Every single act is sacred, formal, and meaningful. By accomplishing such a massive and abundant event, MamaG has been successful in honoring her husband. She will later return home to her endless work and her busy city but, for now, she can be with those in the village and communally honor PapaG.

WITH(IN)

With(in) started as the thesis proposal of master's candidate, Gabriela (Gabi) Bílá Advincula. Gabi, an architect and designer from Brasília, proposed a question to herself and to her community at MIT: is there a connection between the act of procuring food, preparing food and eating together, that can tell us something important about the communities in which we live? Gabi's question quickly became entangled in the group's research theme, titled *The Power of WITHOUT*. *The Power of WITHOUT* acknowledges that by 2050, 3.5 billion people may live in informal settlements without access to conventional infrastructure and buildings. Researchers at MIT are challenged to imagine a future *without* increasingly obsolete heavy infrastructure and *with* lightweight autonomous systems. Gabi's interest in the qualitative exploration of meals in various global communities seemed to fit in well to the group's research direction, and with a rough framework, she set out to meet people in the three communities discussed above.

The MIT team reached out to contacts from various collaborations in each location and were able to connect Gabi with local hosts to welcome her and introduce her to each context and culture. In addition, she worked with local film crews, which contributed added expertise to both the cinematography of the piece and helped to navigate cultural nuances. Each of these hosts and crew members were critical to the success of the piece.

The team wanted to be connected with a community leader in each location, and by chance, the leader suggested in each location was a woman. Eva, Gihan, and MamaG live worlds apart and each lead unique, vibrant lives, yet their leadership implies a commonality. Many qualities are seen in all three women: dignity, compassion, care, resilience, and the trust of those around them. We hope that by sharing this work with the community at the 17th International Architecture Exhibition, this project can provide value and insight as we explore an increasingly complex and undefined world. We believe that Eva, Gihan, and MamaG act as points of inspiration to those in their community, to our team at MIT, and now hopefully to you as well.

At MIT, our work is far from complete, and we are further rocked by the pandemic, looming climate change, and political and social unrest. As *With(in)* teaches us, we need to continue to learn, listen, and document. Our perspective and our understanding will continue to evolve, and with it, new projects will emerge.

MIT Media Lab City Science group, With(in), *Fufu, tamales, and peas, 2020. Image collage.*

following: MIT Media Lab City Science group, With(in), *2020. Installation view.*

MIT Media Lab City Science group

Mexico/

MIT Media Lab
City Science group

Mexico/

ADDENDUM

The above stories were captured from December 2019 to February of 2020. Shortly after this work was completed, the world was faced with the COVID-19 pandemic.
Our team was grateful to have an opportunity to share these stories and gather this content before the pandemic.
We had an opportunity to catch up with the women in the fall of 2020 to learn more about their experiences and the impact of this pandemic on their lives.

Eva

When we caught up with Eva, we learned that she continues to be a key leader in her community. COVID-19 caused chaos throughout Guadalajara as people tried to cope and understand the pandemic. In the midst of this chaos, families in Lomas lost access to their water supply, a supply they used to illegally divert from the main pipes that run around the borders of the community. Eva organized a protest in front of the city hall, and as a result, the government sent a few water trucks for the community to use during quarantine.

In addition, Eva now has a router and a laptop so communication was easier than expected. When asked if she is afraid of contracting COVID-19, Eva said: "*Yo no tengo miedo a nada. Yo soy bien valiente.*" (I fear nothing. I'm very brave.)

Gihan

The Dawar Kitchen is slowly and steadily recovering from a strike. During the strike, the business lost almost all of its important clients. In addition, due to the pandemic, there were no more events to cater. This, coupled with people's bias against and fear of food cooked in poor communities, has made for a very challenging time. The kitchen used their savings to allow the women to stay at home for the worst three months of the pandemic, and later pivoted their business to cater for families with children studying from home.

PROJECT CREDITS

Kent Larson, Gabriela Bílá Advincula, and the City Science group at the MIT Media Lab with Markus Elk ElKatsha, Leticia Izquierdo, Cristina Panzarini, Suleiman Alhadidi, Ariel Noyman, and

Mexico/

The kitchen, which already had very high standards of hygiene, is now even more rigorous. The women have to keep physical distance while cooking and the big communal meal, the happiest part of the day, is unfortunately suspended until further notice.

Gihan stopped working at the kitchen. She has a new partner, someone she might want to marry, and he does not want her to work. Her children continue to do well despite the hardships of the pandemic.

MamaG

MamaG's son set up a video call on his cell phone so we could talk. The internet connection was very limited, but after a few attempts we were able to see MamaG's smiling face. It was late at night and she was coming home from work. The Flyover Market had just reopened after months of shutdown. The government closed every big street market in Port Harcourt, without offering any alternative for people to survive. Illegal night markets started to pop up around the city. MamaG would go to one such market to buy her food, leaving at 2 a.m. and carrying a torch to light her way. If the police were to catch her, she would either have to bribe them or would face getting arrested, but she was covert and able to sneak through successfully. When asked if she is afraid of contracting COVID-19 MamaG said, "No. I'm very healthy. God is taking good care of us."

Jason Nawyn; With(in) protagonists: *Eva (Mexico), Gihan (Egypt) and MamaG (Nigeria);* Nonprofits: *Dawar Kitchen, Ruwwad, Círculo de Amigos Treffpunkt, Universidad de Guadalajara, Chicoco Cinema;* Film: *Ashley Fell and Charles de Graaf (Guadalajara, Mexico), Menna El-Azzamy, Sarah Riad (Cairo, Egypt), and Ana Bonaldo, Michael Uwemedimo, Gloria Dandison, Grace Timi, Imanny Cleverstone, Prince Peter, Promise Sunday, Tammy Dasetima, Tekena Fubara (Port Harcourt, Nigeria), Lucas Seixas, Pedro Ribeiro (Brasilia, Brazil);* Music: *Holger Prang (Hamburg, Germany)*

City Science group at the MIT Media Lab

Egypt/Nigeria

Housing the Future: A New "New Law" for New York City

Daisy Ames,
Bernadette Baird-Zars,
Adam Frampton,
Ericka Mina Song,
Erin Purcell, and
Juan Sebastian Moreno,
The Housing Lab,
Columbia University GSAPP

New

The Housing Lab at Columbia University's Graduate School of Architecture, Planning and Preservation proposes that the parallel crises of inequality and climate change facing New York City today flow through housing to provide a powerful avenue for new models of how we live together. Our proposition is that housing must advance *resilience, inclusion,* and *access* and that a multidisciplinary design approach is required to make real change. We extract elements from a unique moment of housing production at the turn of the last century and create novel combinations for housing in the future.

Located between a river and an ocean, New York City urgently requires new modes of thinking to address the risks from increasing temperatures and natural disasters. We outline *resilient* elements of historic housing projects, such as local material sourcing and passive cooling designs, that offer new potential for adaptation in the city today. Resilience for the Housing Lab is grounded in the hypothesis that good design for dwelling units, buildings, and urban networks can transform possibilities for climate adaptation and mitigation.

Systems of housing across New York City inherited social, political, and economic inequalities that still affect where and how we live—and often also *who* counts in designs and plans. Our installation critically situates unusual spaces of inclusion from forward-thinking designs, codes, and organizational structures, where residents, especially immigrants, seniors, and low-income households were integral to the process and form. Building from these findings, we propose new models and put forth an *inclusive* agenda for affordable housing that is decent and resilient.

To be able to even live in the city and connect to jobs, services, and quality environments is impossible for many New Yorkers. Intersecting scales of infrastructure, services, and finance continue to reinforce neighborhood isolation, financial insecurity, and dislocation. We look to the past to understand how and when housing was affordable and *accessible* in well-designed spaces connected to the city, and argue that novel recombinations of past tools and regulations can unlock the city as a space for everyone.

 York

TOWARD A NEW "NEW LAW"

New York City contains a multitude of housing typologies throughout its five boroughs, most of which have been understood as a generic backdrop to the tall and slender buildings that define the skyline. The multidisciplinary Housing Lab argues that these overlooked buildings embody complex legacies that remain critical for the future of living together. Our goals for this project are twofold: 1) to extract elements from overlooked housing projects that have unique assemblies of materials, design, code, morphology, maintenance, and finance; and 2) to recast selected elements into climate-adaptive and future-oriented outputs that hold promise for new models of living for inclusion, resilience, and access.

In 1901, a broad-reaching Tenement House Act, often called the "New Law," shaped a citywide boom in construction of small and medium buildings of four to six stories that embodied early twentieth-century ideas about improved light and air. Through their abundance, the New Law tenements and other overlooked typologies represent a unique socio-historical inheritance with real currency and value within society that provided much of New York City's housing stock.

By extracting elements and assembling a new "kit of parts" from this overlooked housing stock, we aim to develop creative approaches to recast models for future housing and cities, at the intersection of climate resiliency, inclusivity, and design. Our extractions explore the following hypotheses, based on a multidisciplinary investigation that combines perspectives from architecture, urban planning, and real estate development specialists, across six chapters:

Local Materials Engendered Adaptation

At the turn of the century, housing projects were constructed with locally sourced materials—mainly brick from the Hudson Valley, timber from the Adirondacks, and cement from Rosendale. Our hypothesis is that New York City's proximity to these local materials at the turn of the century offered robust material economies. While the city has sought other global methods of acquiring materials in recent history, we are

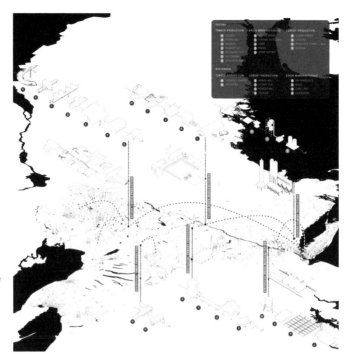

How can historical, regional networks of material sourcing in New York State's Hudson Valley lay the groundwork for material processes in future, low carbon models of construction?

TIMBER PRODUCTION

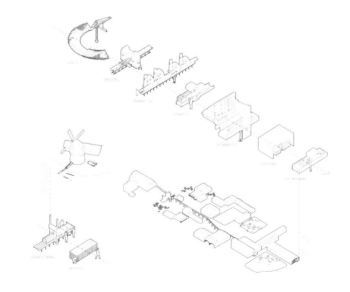

The historical timber production method in the Hudson Valley and its contemporary counterpart.

York

BRICK MANUFACTURING

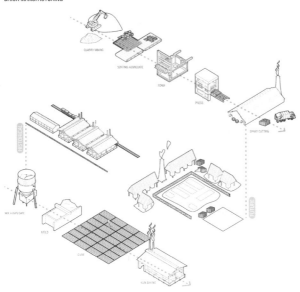

Steps in the historical brick manufacturing process of the Hudson Valley in contrast to contemporary brick manufacturing processes.

CEMENT PRODUCTION

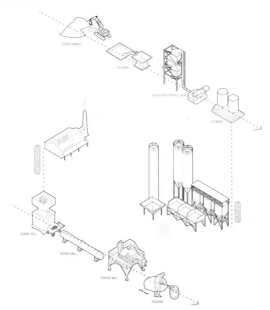

The historical cement production methods employed in the Hudson Valley versus a modernized cement production process.

New

interested in the potential of sourcing materials locally provided our technological innovations, and propose building new models of low-carbon and climate-adaptive housing typologies.

Spatial Organization and Expanded Inclusion
Our research focuses on the interior spatial organization and architectural expression that were made manifest by architects responding to the New Law regulations. At this moment, architects innovated large, light-filled courtyard spaces, open-air stairwells, and intricate ornamentation on building facades to appeal to new regulations in light, air, and beauty. While it is important to acknowledge that demographic and economic lines of exclusion marginalized individuals—namely children, seniors, and low-income families—we see the necessity to revisit some spatial opportunities put forth by Henry Addebury-Smith and Ernest Flagg as efforts to increase community among inhibitors, as this is a need today.

Low-Rise Density Can Enable Broad Access to the City
The New Law tenement projects generated rapid construction of low-rise and high-density urbanism. Without romanticizing the unsafe conditions of the time, our research draws on the historic experience of low-rise density in New York to identify where, how, and why certain densities were able to sustain an improved quality of life, inclusion, and resilience in the city. Beyond the building scale, we illustrate how positive impacts likely hinged on the conditions enabling spaces that can fulfill elements of "home" but that are shared at the building, street, and city level.

Understanding "housing beyond houses" implicates an investigation of how and where housing units were successfully embedded in a broad network of urban services and amenities that were accessible to a wide range of residents. In addition to a spatial inquiry, the installation foregrounds the assemblies of New Law tenements and their intersection with the codes and regulations shaping their urban context and infrastructure and imagines how a "new" New Law could identify neighborhood amenities, broader urban access inclusions, and resilience.

York

New Codes for the City Can Unlock Housing Inclusion

The New Law of 1901 was an ambitious citywide reform to improve housing quality for low- and middle-income households. This law—and the various rules and regulations that followed—have ossified into unwieldy instruments that still powerfully shape the city. The Housing Lab's project at the Biennale investigates specific elements of the ambitious regulation for inclusion and how it came into being, with an emphasis on the coalitions that sustained the rules into practice. As a future-oriented provocation, we outline a proposal for a "new" New Law to address the current housing crisis that would be ambitious, implemented in the public interest, and engage inclusive participation.

First, the research for this installation outlines how far-reaching citywide regulations came into being with the support of particular discourses and coalitions, which then also supervised parts of their implementation. The project attempts to illustrate factors that enabled the adoption and passage of ambitious code, and how these elements might be activated again for a bold regulatory intervention to carry New York beyond 2020.

Further, following the passage of the New Law, we hypothesize that the spaces for exception were also occasionally larger and deployed for the "public interest." While often deployed for wholesale "slum" clearance and systemic displacement, the discretionary tools themselves also made way for workarounds in the zoned densities for affordable housing and large-scale projects. This section of our research questions when, where, and how these spaces of ambition were opened and connected to networks of implementation, and when their processes were inclusive at the design phase.

Lastly, the Lab's installation outlines moments and mechanisms of inclusion when New York's "overlooked" populations, in particular immigrants and seniors, meaningfully shaped the production of housing and neighborhood change. The installation maps elements from these moments that appear to have been key enablers for networks of the "overlooked" in successfully advocating for housing and neighborhood communities; additionally, it tracks a critical understanding of the mutable approaches to "togetherness" and the ways in which inclusion and exclusion changed over time. The Lab also identifies arenas of current code with potential to better include "overlooked" populations.

146

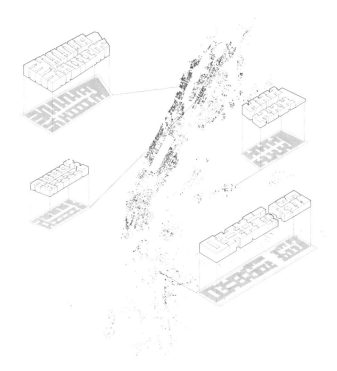

New Law Tenement buildings in New York City, highlighted in dark gray, still comprise a significant portion of the building stock, particularly in Manhattan and The Bronx. These historical blocks may provide a model of density and scale for the future form of the city.

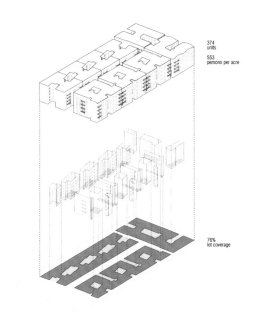

374 units

553 persons per acre

76% lot coverage

The New Law enacted stricter regulations for accessing light and air from all dwelling units. Variations in court, rear and side yard configurations to meet these regulations resulted in the era's distinctive building forms.

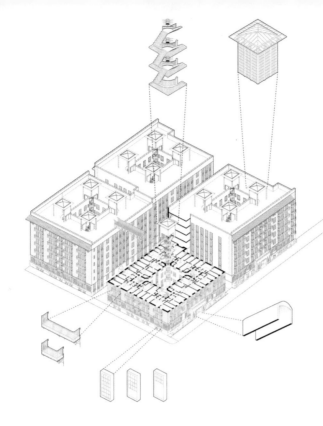

The East River Homes were New Law tenements designed to maximize light and air for tuberculosis patients and their families. The unique spatial innovations created healthy, dignified homes and still remain a case of exemplary architecture in New York City.

The Amalgamated Dwellings was a progressive housing project built to support the nation's labor unions, specifically the Amalgamated Clothing Workers of America. The apartment construction ensured each apartment had views of the street and the interior courtyard, which in turn offered through-apartment ventilation.

New

Housing Only Survives as a Shared And Living Asset
In the face of a housing crisis, many groups of residents self-organized to create structures that could enable more quality housing. While carved along the lines of ethnicity—often at the cost of others—these assemblies still produced thousands of accessible, affordable units and management structures that were relatively independent from state support. From the vantage point of 2019, another moment of high inequality and scarce public resources in cities, the Lab hypothesizes that specific elements of the "overlooked" forms of co-op structures could provide a powerful base for current innovation. With a focus on the Housing Development Finance Corporations (HDFCs) and their physical and organizational potential—which provided and promise particularly inventive models of rethinking the nature of housing as a space for living and doing—the Lab will identify the spaces of opportunity currently in the city.

Developer Diffusion and Proximate Capital Widen Housing Options
To meet demand driven by rapid growth at the turn of the century, countless small firms vied to develop housing in New York City. Drawing on The Housing Lab's interdisciplinary expertise, we investigate if and how meaningful connections exist between the size of a firm and its sources of finance, and the likelihood to develop housing for low and middle-income households. The Lab's installation, in particular, delves into the theorized linkages of greater site specificity, connection to community, and closer-to-the-ground financing sources better able to correctly price the risk of a greater variety of projects. A counterfactual exercise imagines how the New "New Law" could revitalize a broader field of production toward quality and access for the overlooked households and buildings of New York City.

PROJECT CREDITS

Daisy Ames, Bernadette Baird-Zars, and Adam Frampton with Ericka Mina Song, Erin Purcell, Juan Sebastián Moreno, Hyun Hye Bae, Maria E Perez Benavides, Jenna Marie, Kimmel Davis, Lanier Hagerty, Joseph Weil Huennekens, Jin Hong Kim, Yousu Jang, Jiazhen Lin, Adela Locsin, Genevieve Mateyko, Kate McNamara, Zeineb Sellami, Michael Snidal, Angela Sun

The Housing Lab at the Graduate School of Architecture, Planning and Preservation, Columbia University

York

Microcosms and Schisms

Nora Akawi, Hayley Eber,
Lydia Kallipoliti, Lauren Kogod,
and Ife Vanable,
The Irwin S. Chanin School of
Architecture at the Cooper Union

To address how we will live together, we must recognize that *we* refers to a fictive entity, which nonetheless determines a sense of place and kin, and consider the various ways and modes of *living*. A fundamental property of architecture is to demarcate, delineate, and segregate. Faced with processes of differentiation, architecture also registers ruptures and transgressions, and articulates modes of connection and the willful denial of perceived and established boundaries.

In this sense, the urban becomes a constellation of controlled microcosms—carefully constructed spaces of urban interiority and containment of climates, ecologies, and bodies. This installation presents critical readings of such New York interiorities, and the transgressions and breaches that characterize them: the facade and the politics of the envelope, the public park as a space of manufactured wilderness and urban collectivity, spaces of climatic control and streams of waste, and the city's sites of sanctuary and transnational solidarity.

DEEP SEGREGATION
Through readings of the subtle and deeply embedded particularities of the facade as architectural production and materiality, discourse, reality, and mythologies of difference, convention and assembly are implicated as preexisting and ongoing modes of architectural interference and effect. What might a reckoning (both historical and speculative) with fenestration ratios, or window-to-wall ratios, generate in terms of the recognition of the politics of the envelope, and reveal about who constitutes the *we* in terms of who we are and how we live?

PARKS AND RECREATION
As housing tends to segregate rather than integrate, it is mostly outdoors that the most extreme differences coexist. This section of Riverside Park will provide synchronic topographic, geological, and infrastructural information overlaid with projections of diachronic micronarratives. The installation will show cooperation, the "parallel play" constituting public space, as well as covert and overt conflicts.

York

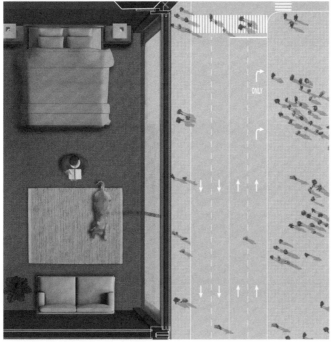

Sally Chen, Nienying Lin, Microcosms and Schisms, *Deep Segragation,* 2020.

The Irwin S. Chanin School of Architecture at the Cooper Union

Giedre Darskute, Jamie Lindsey, Roni Schanin, Microcosms and Schisms, *Parks and Recreation, 2020.*

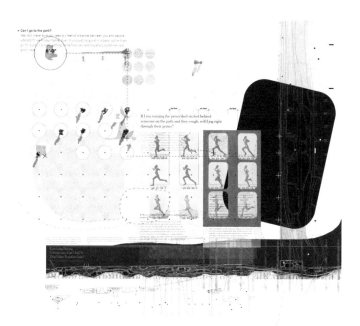

Jamie Lindsey, Microcosms and Schisms, *Parks and Recreation, 2020.*

MICROCLIMATES

Spending 90% of our lives indoors has proliferated as
a modality for living and working in corporate office environments in New York City since the early 1980s. The "Dome
Over Manhattan" is no longer a lost utopia. It is a real, profit-
able proposition for climatically controlled interiors that
reflects the hubris of late-stage capitalism in the heightened
combination of entertainment and ecology within a place
of work. Designing, monitoring, and managing indoor climates
is not only a key engineering project; it also revives a postwar
utopian project, to temper and fabricate the environment as
a site of architectural production. The voluntary containment
of bodies and psyches inside exhibits new forms of urbanization and collectives enabled by the economic and societal
structures of uninhibited energy expenditure. The intention
is to monitor, analyze, and speculate on an indoors that repro-
duces fully controlled sections of the natural world, and further, to critique where we are placed within broader histories
of environmentalism, urbanization, and politics, as well as
how to allow civic agency that enables new forms of economic
and political relations.

SANCTUARY SPACES

Present-day resistance to deportation has been led in
large part by faith organizations and cultural or academic
institutions that draw from a long tradition of granting sanctuary. Urban sanctuaries today constitute the spatial instances
in which the city dissociates itself from national policies and is
activated to work against violations of immigration and refugee
rights. While sanctuary spaces are spaces of enclosure, they
are motivated by the granting of access to safety, resources,
and belonging. While creating protected spaces for persecuted
undocumented groups, sanctuary spaces undermine fortifica-
tions of national borders and the distributed networks of the
police state.

New

*Doosung Shin, Qicheng
Wu,* Microcosms
and Schisms,
Microclimates, 2020.

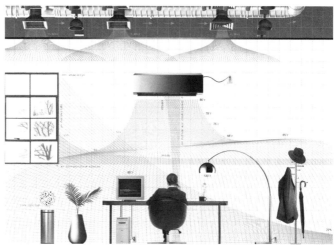

Xiaoxiao Zhao,
Microcosms
and Schisms,
Microclimates, 2020.

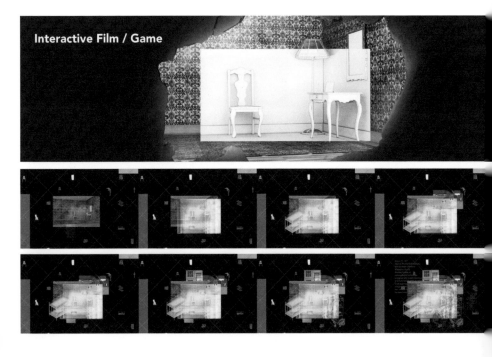

Interactive Film / Game

The scope of this project is to examine how spatial contracts are formed and sustained, as well as what forms of living they engender in New York. In conducting our analysis and design projections, we consider that *New York City is radiated by microcosms.* Among other things, in *Delirious New York* Rem Koolhaas argues against history. To be more explicit, he does not argue against history as evidence, but in the understanding of the city as the passage of time registered on the body of the city, in layers. Unlike a European city that is bound to its history and layered existence, like a palimpsest, New York is defined by the ever-changing present. New York, therefore, is a collection of worlds. Many small worlds exist within any domain of the city as evident in the Madelon Vriesendorp's representation of the "City of the Captive Globe." The Globe is the only object that confers the status of "city" on an otherwise indefinite distension of blocks. It is an idealized version of the city's center or the existence of multiple radiating points instead of a center. The city therefore is not defined by its connections in a continuous field, but rather by its microcosms that radiate in the city from the inside.

The microcosms were selected for their evocative ability to narrate the city. However, throughout the course of this project, our lives have changed "outside-in" within the short course of ten days. The abrupt global response to the spread of COVID-19 radically altered the ways in which we engage with reality and the way we occupy the city. This historic turn of events has signaled a rare, united reflection on the fragility of our production processes, our hubris for ceaseless growth, endless mobility, and finally our accountability as to how we occupy our planet. At the same time, it turned the city inwards, into singular zones of voluntary containment—arrays of immersive territories that can be experienced, crossed and inhabited. New order is generated from collections of inner spaces between individual mental realms of domesticity and the outside.

Austin McInnis,

Yingxiao Chen,

Microcosms and

Schisms, *Sanctuary*

Spaces, 2020

PROJECT CREDITS

Nora Akawi, Hayley Eber,

Lydia Kallipoliti, Lauren

Kogod, Ife Vanable with

Austin Wade Smith,

Pamela Cabrera Pardo,

Eduardo Rega, Ziad

Jamaleddine, Xiaoxiao

Zhao, Niki Kourti, Sally

Chen, Yingxiao Chen,

Nienying Lin, Jamie

Lindsey, Austin McInnis,

Doosung Shin

The Irwin S. Chanin

School of Architecture at

the Cooper Union

York

Prishtina ~~Public~~ Archipelago

Bekim Ramku

Drone image oversee-ing the Grand Hotel, Kino Armata, Rilindja Printhouse, and the Boro-Ramiz Palace of Youth and Sports.

Prish

tina

When one visits Prishtina, particularly during the summer months, one can easily understand how its center lives up to the reputation of a party city. As a country with the youngest population in Europe, the city is the economic, educational, and cultural center of Kosovo, its visiting diaspora, and with many public amenities and social spaces being located centrally, it's not difficult to understand why it is dubbed as such.

But for this part of the city to serve as a social condenser, several political events had to unfold: from the architecturally manifested politics of socialist Yugoslavia, to the creation of the Privatization Agency of Kosovo by the UN protectorate, to the establishment of independent Kosovo institutions, a number of events played an important role in shaping this part of the city.

The study of socialist-era public infrastructure withstanding the test of time in serving its purpose is a recurrent theme lately in many ex-Yugoslav states; however, because of its scale, proximity, and recent regime changes, Prishtina is an ideal case study, relevant not only to regional cities but also to global post-conflict cities.

Since the end of the 1980s, which saw the breakup of ex-Yugoslavia, during the regimes of Serbia and Montenegro, Serbia, and later the UNMIK (United Nations Mission in Kosovo), no public spaces were planned or built in the city. Prishtina today thrives through the (re)use of socialist-era public infrastructure. Its centrally located squares, halls, and centers are used for festivals, markets, arts, music, and other public events.

The object of this study is the center of the city and some of the spaces that contribute to the uncertainty about what is defined as public space in Prishtina, as well as how these spaces serve as perfect grounds for social cohesion. The Boro-Ramiz Palace of Youth and Sports, the Rilindja Printing House, the Grand Hotel, the JNA (Jugoslav National Army) headquarters, the Brotherhood and Unity Square, Mother Theresa Boulevard, as well as the university campus are all spaces of the city that form the Prishtina Public Archipelago.

Bekim Ramku

HOW IT CAME TO BE PUBLIC

Over the last century, Prishtina went through drastic political and cultural changes that not many countries in Europe experienced. In the 1900s Kosovo was ruled by the Ottoman Empire, the Austro-Hungarians, the Bulgarians, Serbia, the Yugoslav Kingdom, the Socialist Federal Republic of Yugoslavia (SFRJ), Serbia and Montenegro, as well as by the UN Mission (UNMIK). All of the above had a great influence on the cultural kaleidoscope that makes up Kosovo today. Architecturally speaking, they all left traces in the local built fabric, be it in urban or rural settings. If one can credit the Ottomans for the mosques, baths, Ottoman-style urban houses; the Austro-Hungarians for the National Museum building; the Bulgarians for the train station; and the UN Mission in Kosovo for the uncontrolled boom in illegal constructions; it is the period of Socialist Yugoslavia that can be credited for the creation of public space in the form of squares, housing projects complimented with adequate green and recreational spaces, and cultural and sports venues.

Post-WWII Prishtina was still a small Ottoman-style setting and it took several decades for the city to see the kinds of investments that were underway in other larger urban centers around ex-Yugoslavia. It was in late 1959 and early 1960 that Prishtina got its first "proper" square—meaningfully named the "Brotherhood and Unity Square." It featured a central obelisk depicting pointed air rifles and bronze sculptures of partisan soldiers helping each other. The square was constructed at the location where the Prishtina Bazaar used to be and became an instant city landmark, more for its ideological obelisk and sculptures than for its spatial qualities. Later the square was used for large public gatherings and speeches such as Marshal Tito and Slobodan Milošević's.

In the late 1960s the Yugoslav government agreed on opening the first Albanian-speaking university in the country, and in the '70s and '80s large housing complexes were being built throughout Prishtina. The capital city and the new autonomous province of Kosovo needed public infrastructure that could accommodate the rising needs of the modern socialist society.

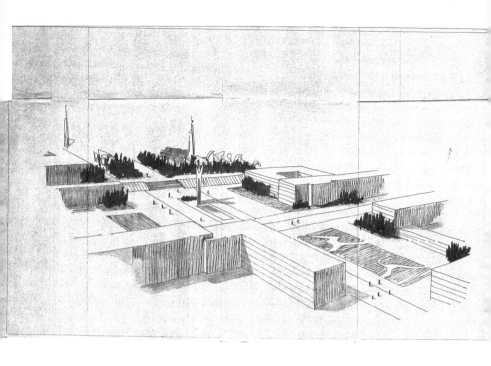

*Sketch of the Bashkim
Vllaznimi (Brotherhood
and Unity) square.*

162   *Bekim Ramku*

Right after the Yugoslav government agreed to establish the University of Prishtina in 1969, the prominent Kosovar architect Bashkim Fehmiu was given the task of planning the new campus. Fehmiu, who was a delegate and follower of CIAM, planned for a mat-like structure to cover the whole of the centrally located campus, leaving larger internal open courts where the university library and the main open amphitheater would be located. As a grand gesture to inaugurate the university, local authorities decided to first construct the university library, which was designed by the Croatian Andrija Mutnjaković and took more than a decade to be finished. The campus, on the other hand, still remains unfinished according to Fehmiu's masterplan.

The 1970s saw the start of the construction on the Rilindja Printing House, the Boro-Ramiz Palace of Youth and Sports, the Grand Hotel, the JNA headquarters, as well as the large neighborhoods of Ulpiana, Kurrizi and Bregu i Diellit. Prishtina was rapidly undergoing spatial changes that would provide the missing physical and social infrastructure needed for a progressive urban setting.

Boro-Ramiz was planned as a social condenser on steroids, a blown-up version of the "Zadruga" that would accommodate all of the recreational, cultural, and social needs of the new capital.[1] The project, which was designed by the Bosnian architecture group composed of Živorad Janković, Halid Muhasilović and Srećko Espek, was never fully finished. Interestingly, 70% of the funds for its construction were secured by Kosovo citizens in the form of salary contributions, while the 30% which was supposed to be secured by the Yugoslav central government never came through, thus the auxiliary spaces of the swimming pool and open sports courts were never realized. The center offered predominantly free sports activities throughout the 1980s during the Milosević's rule and the apartheid of the 1990s, but banned access to its sports and cultural spaces to Albanians.

1   "Zadruga" is what the locals in Yugoslavia called the "Zadruzni Domovi," a model imported from farming cooperatives in the USSR known as "Uzadruge," Usually the cooperatives functioned as more than just a space for them, and in many instances the structures had a broader program including movie theaters, ambulance, grocery stores, etc. See Jelena Živančević, "Soviet in Content—People's in Form: The Building of Farming Cooperative Centers and the Soviet-Yugoslav Dispute, 1948–1950," *SPATIUM International Review*, no. 25 (September 2011): 39–49.

But it is the latter period of the UNMIK rule and the Kosovo Privatization Agency (KPA) management that created the perfect grounds for larger venues to remain publicly undefined.[2]

THE STATE OF PUBLICNESS

With the urge to sell assets, or in the case of Rilindja, Boro-Ramiz, and the Grand Hotel, to rent them, KPA started fragmenting and renting spaces without consideration for their original use and the social values these spaces represented. The Rilindja Printing House, designed by the Macedonian architect George Konstantinovski, was originally the seat of the largest daily Kosovar newspapers in Albanian, Serbo-Croatian, and Turkish. Now the Rilindja building is half owned by the Kosovo Government, while the other half is "squatted" by TV stations, news websites, coffee shops, restaurants, night clubs, gyms, etc.

The largest hotel in the city, the Grand Hotel was at one point privatized. The "asset" was sold to local businessmen under the condition that they invest a certain amount of funds and preserve its original use. In a very publicized set of events, with the excuse that the new owners hadn't invested the promised funds, the hotel returned to KPA management. Later, the new owners accused KPA of bribery, and months later the KPA director committed suicide. Since 2012, the Grand is managed by the KPA, but the investors made sure to leave their mark on the building by striping one tower of the hotel of its interior and covering its facade in aluminum panels.

Once the "pride" of the city, it is now in a very bad state, at least visually speaking, and has even been named the worst hotel in the world by the *New York Times*.[3] Today, covered by billboards, the Grand houses several coffee shops, restaurants,

2 The Kosovo Privatization Agency (KPA) is an agency that manages the privatization of all publicly owned assets. The KPA is viewed by the general public as a corrupt and mismanaged agency, which has, since its establishment in 2002, generated more than 700 million euros, which it invested in foreign stocks. See the Kosovo Privatization Agency's website, accessed March 15, 2021, http://www.pak-ks.org/page.aspx?id=2,1.

3 Andrew Higgins, "Not the Worst Hotel in the World, Perhaps, but 'the World Is Very Big'," *New York Times*, March 1, 2018, https://www.nytimes.com/2018/03/01/world/europe/kosovo-grand-hotel.html.

Bekim Ramku

Prish

Boro-Ramiz Palace of

Youth and Sports

during construction.

travel agencies, souvenir shops, a gym, a hotel, and a club on the thirteenth floor. But its main attraction is still Tito's room, which requires special permission to visit from the KPA. Boro-Ramiz is a similar case, although at its core, the center had three key uses: recreational, educational and cultural, and commercial. Under KPA management, its program was further fragmented and was manifested spatially with the opening of schools, clubs, and theatres, which meant spaces were subdivided by putting up new brick or plasterboard walls.

Spatial developments of recent decades in Prishtina included urban sprawl, gated communities, informal construction, privatization of public space, and large housing blocks and neighborhoods without any consideration for public space. All of these developments have an effect on the socio-economic and cultural divisions in the city on a level never witnessed before. To protect and nourish public space is a fight that has to be won by the city and its citizens. Prishtina's city center should be used as a study on publicness and how this idea could be replicated in other parts of the city or the country facing similar issues.

Recently there have been positive changes. On the initiative of the Prishtina mayor, Boro-Ramiz was declared an asset of national importance. After being removed from the KPA privatization list, its debt was paid, and it was returned to city management.[4] It is still unclear what the city will do with Boro-Ramiz and how they will incorporate its current uses in their future plans for the venue. Yet, one thing is certain: the center, which was engulfed by a fire that destroyed its large sports hall some fifteen years ago, won't be demolished. Several years ago, the proposed project by the European Commission to knock down the center and build a new one based on the original program was badly received. In a recent interview, the mayor vowed to return the center to its former glory by rebuilding the hall that had burned and constructing the unfinished parts of the complex.

4 Kushtrim Hajzeri, "Ky është plani i Shpend Ahmetit për 'Boro e Ramizi'n," Media Ndërtimi, September 30, 2017, https://ndertimi.info/ky-eshte-plani-i-shpend-ahmetit-per-boro-e-ramizin/.

top: Grand Hotel façade.

bottom: Interior of the Grand Hotel, incomplete refurbishment work, 2020.

167

above and opposite:
Tito's room, the room
where Marshall Tito slept
when he visited Prishtina,
the space kept most of
its original design and
is a touristic attraction,
Grand Hotel.

right: *Basement space*
originally used
for bowling, Grand
Hotel, 2020.

Bekim Ramku Prish

left: View of the damaged large hall of Boro-Ramiz Palace of Youth and Sports.

below: Interior of the Rilindja print house after it was occupied by KPA (Kosovo Privatization Agency).

Bekim Ramku

Prish

In 2019, the city also acquired another iconic socialist-era landmark: the Gërmia Shopping Mall. After a lengthy debate over its regeneration or demolition, the city decided to keep the building and use it for public needs, most likely for a cultural center.[5]

There are also plans to pedestrianize the George Bush Street which will make the Mother Theresa Boulevard—the existing central pedestrian artery—stretch all the way to the cathedral which bears her name, as well as connect the central boulevard even further to the campus.

Several nonprofit organizations are also looking at ways to squat spaces within the core of the center, with the hope that the Privatization Agency will find it difficult to sell the asset once the potential privatizers learn that the spaces are occupied.

The cinema of the ex-Yugoslav National Army's HQ is now managed by an NGO and has been renamed to "Kino Armata."[6] Now a public cinema and event space, for a symbolic amount it hosts large and small cultural events such as the Redo Design Conference, the Prishtina International Film Festival, the Kosovo Architecture Festival, music and poetry nights, and of course screenings of independent films. Another NGO called Hapësira organizes electronic music events and uses the money to help underprivileged families is managing part of the Rilindja Printing House and planning to make it a permanent space for a cultural center.[7]

With all of the political ambiguity and socio-economic issues that Kosovo and its capital city face today, the Prishtina Public Archipelago study aims to serve as a guideline of possibilities and transmit to visitors some of the positivity that comes with the socio-cultural activation of these spaces.

5   Cristina Marí, "'Gërmia' Controversy Signals Divisions on How to Grow Prishtina," Kosovo 2.0, October 24, 2018, https://kosovotwopoint zero.com/en/germia -controversy-signals -divisions-on-how-to -grow-prishtina/.

6   Plator Gashi, "Yugoslav-Era Cinema Reopens its Doors in Prishtina," *Prishtina Insight*, April 25, 2018, https:// prishtinainsight.com /yugoslav-era-cinema -reopens-doors -prishtina-mag/.

7   Hapësira's Facebook page, accessed March 15, 2021, https:// www.facebook.com /hapesirahapesira/.

PROJECT CREDITS

Bekim Ramku with

Nol Binakaj

Kosovo Architecture

Foundation

RIO DE JANEIRO

How Rio
Lived
Together

Sérgio Burgi,
Farès el-Dahdah,
Alida C. Metcalf,
and David Heyman

Rio de Janeiro's harbor
and customs house,
c. 1865.

How we *will* live together is deeply tied to how we *have* lived together. Our digital time machine, *imagineRio,* invites contemplation of urban social spaces, both lived and imagined, over five hundred years.

The first social spaces of Rio de Janeiro were the fort, the church, and irregularly spaced dwellings in a natural open space. The setting was magnificent—the top of a hill overlooking a beautiful bay with a dense forest extending up the steep slopes of hills, topped with exposed granite peaks. The fort and the church symbolized the intertwined ambitions of the Portuguese Crown: the fort to claim and hold the territory, the Jesuit church to evangelize native peoples and to succor colonists. The space in front of the church and around the fort served as an informal public square where residents circulated in rhythms set by daily life, festivals marked in the religious calendar, and the arrival and departure of ships. The space was open to all, but not all were equal. A visible and highly stratified social hierarchy characterized Rio from the beginning.

As Rio grew, it moved from the hill into a more regularized, planned space along the beach. A long rectangular grid of streets perpendicular to the shoreline extended back between four hills. Narrow and paved with stone, the streets of Rio conveyed the necessities of daily life and the business of the port. The beach linked the streets to the bay. It was not then a place for leisure or recreation. Local boatmen landed their crafts piled with foodstuffs for the markets and street vendors. The sailors of oceangoing ships unloaded their cargoes and reprovisioned their ships. Africans, forced into slaving ships on the other side of the Atlantic, came ashore to be auctioned off. At night the beach was a dark place where garbage, waste, and night soil was dumped for the tide to carry away.

All cities need water, but Rio was not located on a river. At the back of the city, the first fountain began to flow in 1723. Fed by a long aqueduct that extended up into the Tijuca Forest, the fountain had been designed and its stones cut in Portugal.

top: Jean Baptiste Debret, Ash Wednesday Morning at Church, *1816–1832.*

bottom: Jean Baptiste Debret, View of the Palace Square in Rio de Janeiro, *1816–1832.*

following spread: Luís dos Santos Vilhena, Map of the City of Saint Sebastien of Rio de Janeiro, *1775.*

Sérgio Burgi, Farès el-Dahdah, Alida C. Metcalf, and David Heyman

Rio de

UNE MATINÉE DU MERCREDI SAINT, À L'ÉGLISE.

VUE DE LA PLACE DU PALAIS, À RIO DE JANEIRO.

aneiro

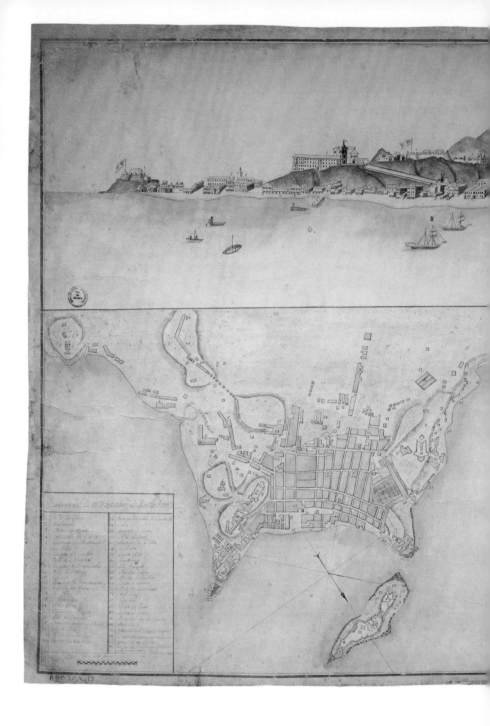

Sérgio Burgi, Farès el-Dahdah,
Alida C. Metcalf, and David Heyman

Rio de

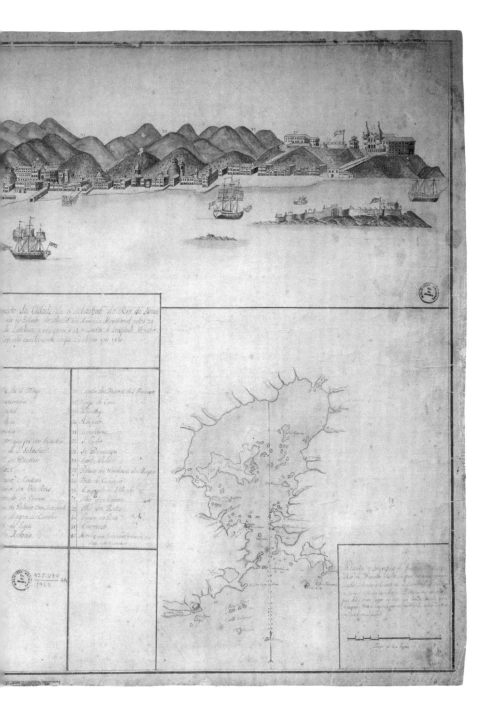

right: Largo da Carioca Foundation, c. 1890.

below: Carioca Aqueduct, also known as Lapa Arches, 1905.

Sérgio Burgi, Farès el-Dahdah, Alida C. Metcalf, and David Heyman Rio de

Once assembled, the square in front of it became a crowded place. Tasked with collecting water, enslaved laborers rose early to fill their vessels. As they waited, they exchanged news, made acquaintances, and spoke in their native languages. Sometimes fights broke out and so too did music. Carrying water was hard and endless. The city councilors hired a guard to keep order, but enslaved men and women made the square their own. As the aqueduct fed more fountains, similar patterns unfolded in the public spaces surrounding them.

The main square that opened to the bay was a simple place until Rio became the capital of the colony in 1763. The square was redesigned to allow soldiers to parade in front of the governor's palace, which stood along one side. The surface of the square was paved with sparkling stones, and the fountain moved to a new sea wall where ships could easily fill their water casks.

Other squares also changed. The Campo dos Ciganos, named for the first Romani to arrive in Rio, gradually became a central enclosed square, known as Rossio. In one corner stood the *pelourinho*, the brutal whipping post found in all Portuguese cities. The Campo de Santa Anna at the back of the city served as an open commons where cattle and horses were pastured. In the early nineteenth century, its fountain became the primary work site for laundresses. In time it would be landscaped into a park. In the beginning, there were few parks. The first, the Passeio Público, took the place of the Boqueirão Lagoon after it was drained in the eighteenth century.

When the royal court, fleeing Napoleon, arrived in 1808, the prince regent, with his aged mother, the Queen, and the rest of the royal family took up residence on the central square. The nearby church of the Carmo Convent became the royal chapel where royal family events, as well as momentous political transitions, took place, such as the acclamation of King João VI. Later, Quinta da Boa Vista became the royal residence outside of the central city, in São Cristóvão.

The Valongo Wharf, designated as the slave market by an eighteenth-century Vice Roy—who determined that its sordid business should take place out of sight of the central

city—lay north. Thousands of slaves continued to arrive until the slave trade was declared illegal in 1830.

Although the warehouses in the Valongo shut, an illegal slave trade continued. Even after the transatlantic trade ceased in 1850, enslaved men and women still arrived in Rio through an internal trade. Coming from the economically depressed northeast, these men and women passed along streets and through auction houses on their forced journeys to the coffee fazendas of São Paulo.

Yellow fever became the scourge of Rio in the second half of the nineteenth century. When ships avoided landing, public officials sought a solution in vain. Unlike smallpox, against which officials had been vaccinating since colonial times, or leprosy, which sent patients to quarantine on an island in the bay, yellow fever spread mysteriously and with devastating effects on immigrants.

Seeking to eliminate unhealthy air, believed to be the source of disease, city officials planned reforms. Slums would be eliminated, and the city center opened to allow fresh air to circulate. Plans date from the 1840s and the 1870s, but the "Haussmannization" of Rio was the project of Mayor Pereira Passos early in the twentieth century. The mayor created avenues, the most important being the Avenida Central, that cut through the old urban fabric. Wide and lined with new buildings, the avenue projected a new, sophisticated identity for Rio. The demolition of the Morro do Castelo—the site of the first fort and church on top of the hill—soon became inevitable. In its place architects, designers, and builders constructed new buildings in carefully designed spaces. Federal buildings, such as the Senate and the Electoral Tribunal, and the National Library and the Teatro Municipal, were erected. To the south, the Avenida Beira Mar extended, built over new land created from the rubble.

The *cortiços* had offered cheap living arrangements for the poor in the central city. When demolished by city officials, the poor sought new places to live, and many moved up into the hills. The *morros* above the old Valongo had the advantage of being close

top: Municipal Theater of Rio de Janeiro, c. 1910.

bottom: São Domingos Plaza, c. 1910.

Sérgio Burgi, Farès el-Dahdah, Alida C. Metcalf, and David Heyman

Beira Mar Avenue at the

Passeio Público, 1926 .

Sérgio Burgi, Farès el-Dahdah,
Alida C. Metcalf, and David Heyman

Rio de

left: Dismantlment of
Castelo Hill, with the
ruins of Saint Sebastian
Church on top of the
hill, 1922.

below: Aerial view of Rio
de Janeiro, from Mauá
Square to the southern
zone, showing Sugar Loaf
Hill in the background,
c. 1922.

Flamengo landfill, 1966.

*Sérgio Burgi, Farès el-Dahdah,
Alida C. Metcalf, and David Heyman*

Rio de

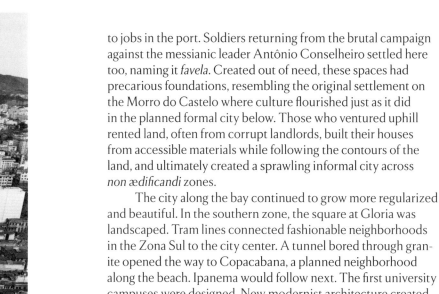

to jobs in the port. Soldiers returning from the brutal campaign against the messianic leader Antônio Conselheiro settled here too, naming it *favela*. Created out of need, these spaces had precarious foundations, resembling the original settlement on the Morro do Castelo where culture flourished just as it did in the planned formal city below. Those who ventured uphill rented land, often from corrupt landlords, built their houses from accessible materials while following the contours of the land, and ultimately created a sprawling informal city across *non ædificandi* zones.

The city along the bay continued to grow more regularized and beautiful. In the southern zone, the square at Gloria was landscaped. Tram lines connected fashionable neighborhoods in the Zona Sul to the city center. A tunnel bored through granite opened the way to Copacabana, a planned neighborhood along the beach. Ipanema would follow next. The first university campuses were designed. New modernist architecture created a distinctly Carioca School, as illustrated by Lucio Costa's Ministry of Education and Health building in 1936. Roberto Burle Marx designed a stunning park along Flamengo that extended the original Avenida Beira Mar. In the world of Burle Marx, one sees what Alice witnessed in Wonderland: sudden shifts in scale, flashes of color, paintings that one can enter. To walk across the wavy patterns on the Copacabana Boardwalk is to simultaneously occupy the space of the surf; to live in one of the adjacent apartment buildings is to perpetually witness a lively public spectacle unfolding below. Driving down this Avenida Atlântica, one simultaneously engages with vistas of people, art created from black and white marble stones (*pedra portuguesa*), architecture, the seashore, prostitutes, joggers, palm trees, and vendors, all stylishly interacting in a compelling landscape. A unique social space transformed *carnaval*, which had always been a street celebration, in the 1980s. Oscar Niemeyer's Sambódromo created a dedicated space for the lavish parade of Samba Schools, but it also served as a school for the rest of the year.

The city progressively attracted migrants from the northeast in the 1950s, '60s, and '70s, leading to an expansion of the

aneiro

Sérgio Burgi, Farès el-Dahdah,
Alida C. Metcalf, and David Heyman Rio de

Street scene,
Rocinha, 2012.

informal communities on the hills. Migrants and locals built simple houses, brick by brick, room by room. Distinctive social spaces appeared, steep stairs and winding alleys, similar to those that once led into the Morro do Castelo. Others, like soccer fields and evangelical churches, had no precedent. Even after being taken over by drug lords in the 1980s, favelas had local leaders who resisted many eradication campaigns. Some were nevertheless forcibly relocated far from the city center in new yet poorly designed neighborhoods. Faced with daily violence caused by both drug wars and police brutality, favela residents engaged in processes of community formation and open public space strategies. Frequently represented as places of scarcity, favelas always stood out as spaces for dense public gathering.

When the capital of Brazil moved from Rio to Brasília in the 1960s, Rio's social spaces lost prestige and revenue but not their iconic appeal or flagrant inequalities. The beaches took on central and powerful new identities as spaces that everyone—from rich to poor—could enjoy. Still, they remained places of work for those who serve the crowds. The modernist aesthetic of the twentieth century continued to transform Rio as new neighborhoods opened, such as Barra da Tijuca, and as Rio became the site for major international events, such as the World Cup and the Olympics.

This visit to the past through *imagineRio* reminds us that social spaces are always emerging, changing, and shaping lives. How we will live together depends on how these spaces are reimagined so that memory and citizenship can face a legacy of challenges, inequalities and contradictions.

PROJECT CREDITS

Farès el-Dahdah, Alida C. Metcalf, David Heyman, Sérgio Burgi with Bruno Sousa, Uilvim Ettore, Ualas Barreto Rohrer, Bruno Buccalon, Lisa Spiro, Ben Sheesley, Andy Woodruff, Martim Passos, Cíntia Mechler, Maiara Pitanga, Naylor Vilas Boas, Asla Medeiros e Sá, Paulo Cezar P. Carvalho, Aruan Braga, Lino Teixeira, Ana Luiza Nobre, Antônio Firmino, Fernando Ermiro, Michel Silva, Luiz Carlos Toledo, Jens Ingensand, Stéphane Lecorney, Nicolas Blanc, Loïc Fürhoff, Timothée Produit

Rice University, Axis Maps, Instituto Moreira Salles, Universidade Federal do Rio de Janeiro, Fundação Getulio Vargas, Observatório de Favelas, Memória Rocinha, Haute École d'Ingénierie et de Gestion du Canton de Vaud

Sérgio Burgi, Farès el-Dahdah, Alida C. Metcalf, and David Heyman

Rio de

*24-hour Health
Care Unit, Estrada da
Gávea, Rocinha, 2012.*

Access for All: São Paulo's Architectural Infrastructures
Daniel Talesnik

Paulo Mendes da Rocha and MMBB Arquitetos (Fernando Mello Franco, Marta Moreira, Milton Braga), Serviço Social do Comércio (SESC) 24 May, *2001–2017, the thirteenth floor rooftop pool, 2019.*

For decades, São Paulo has witnessed investments in architectural infrastructures that help alleviate the lack of public space in the megacity. Many of these projects also provide the city of São Paulo's twelve million inhabitants with access to recreational, cultural, and athletic programs—much-needed resources in this dense metropolis of tremendous inequality, high crime rates, severe traffic issues, and serious public health problems. This abridged version of *Access for All: São Paulo's Architectural Infrastructures* presents a selection of public, public-private, and privately owned, and buildings that attempt to create inclusive places for urban society.[1] The featured projects are presented with a focus on their programmatic characteristics, rather than their formal qualities, which are usually emphasized in scholarship on Brazilian architecture. Regardless of when they were constructed, these projects are analyzed as they stand today, through newly commissioned photographs, films, architectural drawings, illustrations, models, and interviews. *Access for All* looks at how architects working at the building scale design the city incrementally, and conversely, how the accumulated built logic of the city has an impact on its architecture and public spaces. These projects show how architecture weaves in and out of the city, blurring the boundaries between buildings and the public realm. Sidewalks merge into ramps, stairs, and escalators, and at times reappear in the cityscape as elevated or sunken plazas, rooftop terraces, and gardens. While many cities around the world are still chasing the Bilbao effect—the creation of a monofunctional, signature architectural work by a famous architect to attract tourism—*Access for All* advocates for architecture that serves diverse cultural, social, and recreational functions, all aimed at sustaining the needs of São Paulo's residents.

The three selected projects are large multiprogrammatic buildings, which can be grouped under a research category related to the Russian Constructivists' concept of the "social condenser"

1   *Access for All: São Paulo's Architectural Infrastructures* was exhibited at the Architekturmuseum der TUM at the Pinakothek der Moderne in Munich (June 13–September 8, 2019); Center for Architecture, New York (February 11, 2020–February 8, 2022); and, Swiss Architecture Museum, Basel (March 20–August 8, 2021). Centro Cultural São Paulo (CCSP), one of the exhibition case studies, was shown alone at the 12th International Architecture Biennial of São Paulo, CCSP (September 10–December 8, 2019).

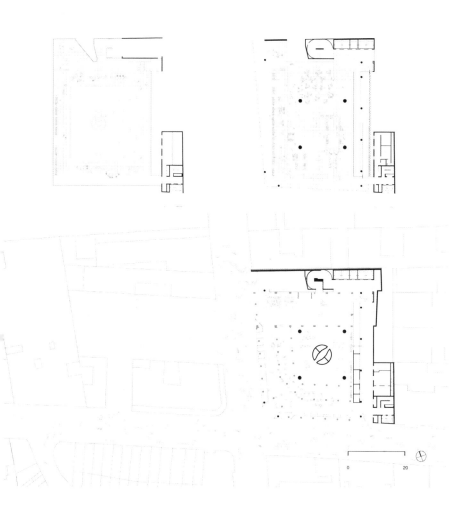

Serviço Social do
Comércio (SESC)
24 May, *2001–2017,
floor plans.*

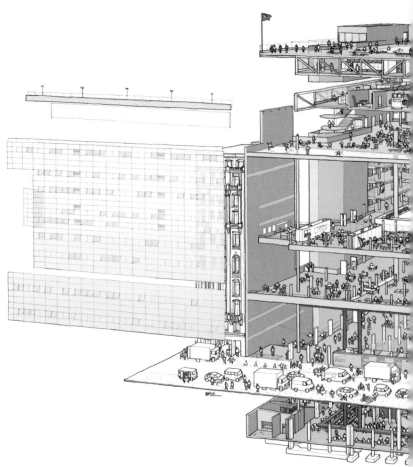

Serviço Social do
Comércio (SESC)
24 May, *2001–2017,*
exploded perspective
drawing.

São

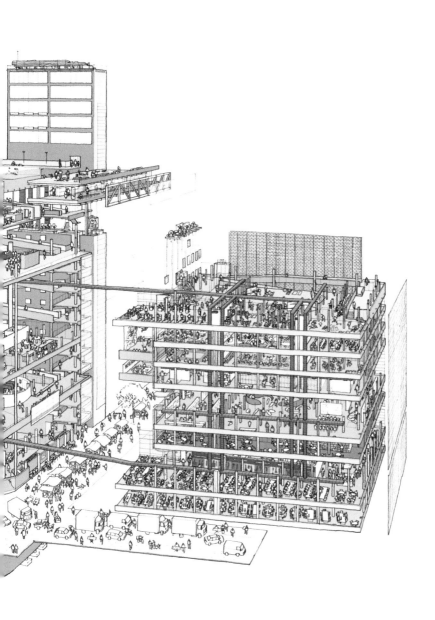

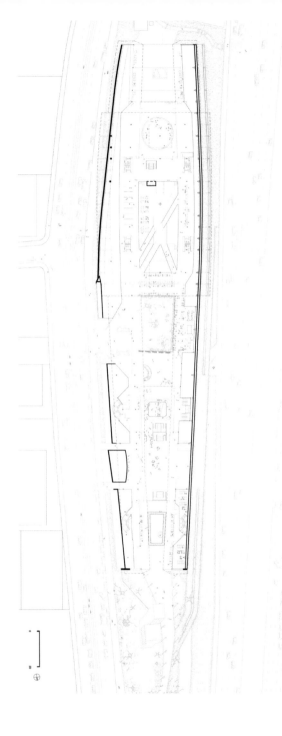

Eurico Prado Lopes and Luiz Telles, Centro Cultural São Paulo (CCSP), *1976–1982.*

following: Centro Cultural São Paulo (CCSP), *1976–1982, dancing in one of the sunken terraces, 2019.*

Daniel Talesnik

in the Soviet Union in the 1920s: buildings such as workers' clubs that had the aim of dynamizing society through sports, culture, and education.[2] If one removes (or makes less explicit) the ideological component of these Soviet examples, it is possible to see the kernel for the Serviço Social do Comércio (SESC) buildings. The SESC buildings—twenty-three in total in the city of São Paulo and forty-three altogether in São Paulo State—deliver an array of recreational, educational, and cultural services to "workers of commerce" in Brazil.[3] While union-owned, the SESC's centers are financed by taxes, state funding, and through users' payments for certain activities. These buildings have proliferated in São Paulo, particularly since the 1960s when the SESC Consolação set the model for the Downtown-Athletic-Club-like approach of these projects. This agglomeration of programs of different natures has seen many variations, including Paulo Mendes da Rocha and MMBB's SESC 24 de Maio, which is the outcome of a complex intervention in a pre-existing building that, together with the addition of a service tower, results in moments like the double-height gymnasium on top of a single-height dentistry service woven together by a side ramp.[4] In all cases, at least one part of their facilities is accessible to the general public free of charge.

Another project in this category is the Centro Cultural São Paulo (CCSP), developed on land that was originally expropriated for the construction of the city's subway. Eurico Prado Lopes and Luiz Telles's design, selected through an open competition held in 1976, nods to this intended use for the site by submerging the project below ground. Construction ran from 1978 through 1982, while Brazil was still under a military dictatorship. While the center has experienced periods of decline, it has been popular with São Paulo's citizens from the start. As of late, it has become a destination for people from all over the city, which is facilitated

2 For more on Constructivist social condensers, see "The Social Condenser: A Century of Revolution Through Architecture, 1917–2017," eds. Michał Murawski and Jane Rendell, special issue, *The Journal of Architecture*, 22, no. 3 (2017).

3 In the United States, for example, the SESCs could be described as a combination between a YMCA, an arts and crafts center, a performing arts center, a food court, and a dental clinic.

4 For more about the Downtown Athletic Club, see Rem Koolhaas, *Delirious New York: A Retroactive Manifesto for Manhattan* (New York: Oxford University Press, 1978).

Daniel Talesnik

Sāo

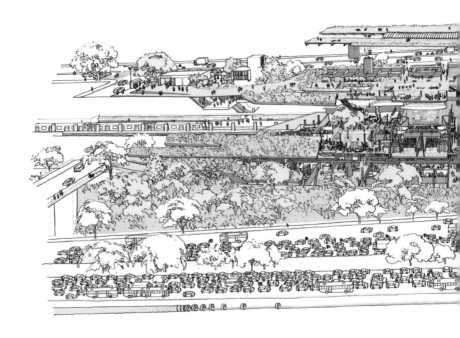

Daniel Talesnik

Sã

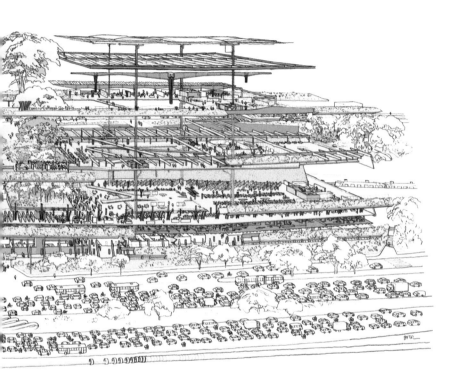

Centro Cultural
São Paulo (CCSP),
*1976–1982, exploded
perspective drawing.*

by CCSP's integration into the city's public transportation system via the Vergueiro subway station. Particularly popular as a library, exhibition space, and lunch spot, CCSP has also become an epicenter for young dance troupes: small groups rehearse their routines throughout the building's public spaces. The maintenance of the building is a critical issue, both in terms of the security of its users and the upkeep of its facilities. As is the case with many heavily trafficked public buildings today, free WiFi is as important as some of the project's physical qualities.

The CCSP is a paradigmatic example of public architecture that straddles the scales of urbanism and architecture.

A more recent addition to this constellation is the Centro Educacional Unificado (CEU) Inácio Monteiro. The Unified Education Center initiative was launched in 2003 to open schools in the most vulnerable districts of São Paulo, many of which are located in the city's periphery. Forty-five CEUs were built between 2003 and 2004 using the same modules and similar configurations across all sites. The CEUs were conceived by Paulo Freire, who served as São Paulo Secretary of Education under the Workers' Party starting in 1989. Architects Alexandre Delijaicov, André Takiya, and Wanderley Ariza gave architectural form to the concept and conducted analyses to determine the location of the centers. Delijaicov refers to the CEUs as "Social Equipment Squares" (Praças de Equipamentos Sociais).

The CEUs, including Inácio Monteiro, anchor their surrounding neighborhoods. Beyond serving as schools, they are community centers, providing day care, adult education classes, sports and recreation spaces, cultural events, and leisure activities. CEUs also house social welfare offices and health facilities. Formally, all CEUs are organized as three distinct, simple volumes. The largest building, an orthogonal grid, houses classrooms, dining rooms, computer rooms, a library, a baking school, and galleries. The disk-shaped volume houses a nursery. The smaller orthogonal building houses a theater, a gymnasium, and a music room.

Alexandre Delijaicov, André Takiya and Wanderley Ariza, Centro Educacional Unificado (CEU) Inácio Monteiro, *2001–2003, ground floor plan.*

following: Centro Educacional Unificado (CEU) Inácio Monteiro, *2001–2003, view of the courtyard, 2019.*

Daniel Talesnik

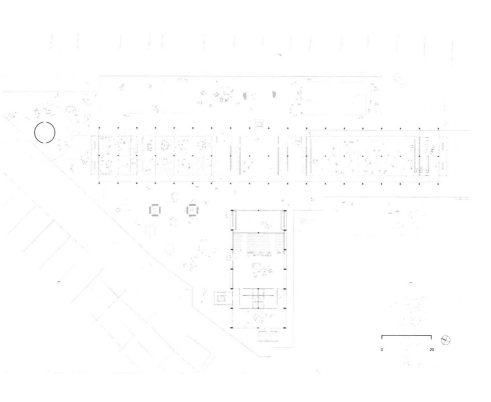

0   20

Daniel Talesnik Sã

Paulo

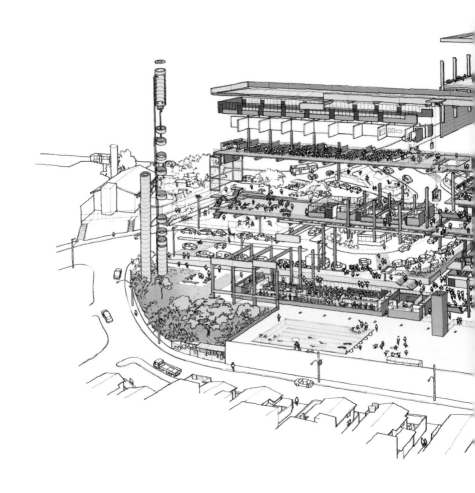

Centro Educacional
Unificado (CEU)
Inácio Monteiro,
*2001–2003, exploded
perspective drawing.*

Sãc

Paulo

If one looks at several of the buildings in the "large multi-programmatic" category, for example the CCSP that is shown in the Venice Biennale installation, or SESC Pompéia that is part of the larger exhibition, they were designed and/or built during the years of the dictatorship in Brazil. Although CCSP does not directly represent the political system under which it was built, it is interesting to see that architecture can be more stable than the system that commissioned and built it. Even in times of repression in São Paulo there was a concern for collective infrastructure, which suggests particularities of the city and its architectural culture.[5] Additionally, these buildings can give perspective and ideas that lend themselves to critical reflection on architecture and the current political moment in Brazil.

Despite the fact that this installation exhibits projects that represent São Paulo's architectural infrastructures and how it is possible to construct the city from within buildings, we are aware that there is a need for more of these kind of infrastructure in such a heavily populated city. Also, with the exception of the CEU network, the examples presented are in the central area of São Paulo. The periphery is different. Different sources provide different data: millions of São Paulo's citizens live in slum-like conditions and a critical number of existing housing faces the reality of landslides and flooding. (Although São Paulo generates over ten percent of Brazil's GDP, conservative estimates establish that a fifth of its population lives in poverty). We started by focusing on existing knowledge about these buildings in São Paulo, and then excavated new evidence to support and illustrate our arguments. We suggest a conception of architecture/architectures that is not only essential to urban processes but also able, at its best, to generate new urban and urbanization processes. This is a reading of architecture that has political undertones and that reaffirms the possible agencies that complexly programmed buildings have in supporting life in cities. It is our ambition that our analyses are useful for cities around the world.

5   See Renato Anelli, "Architecture and Metropolitan Culture: CCSP and SESC Pompéia," in *Access for All: São Paulo's Architectural Infrastructures*, eds. Andres Lepik and Daniel Talesnik (Zurich: Park Books, 2019), 20–25.

PROJECT CREDITS

Daniel Talesnik and

Andres Lepik with

Mariana Vilela, Kathryn

Gillmore, Ciro Miguel,

Pedro Kok, Danilo

Zamboni, Guilherme

Pianca, Gabriel Sepe,

Joao Bittar Fiammenghi,

Marcello Della Giustina,

Pia Nurnberger, Anna

List, Mariana Lourenco,

Anna-Maria Meister,

Andreas Bohmann,

Thomas Lohmaier,

Anton Heine, Guilherme

Pianca, Gabriel Sepe

and team, Danilo

Zamboni, Pedro Kok,

Marta Moreira, Renato

Cymbalista, and

Alexandre Delijaicov,

John Wriedt, Dawn

Michelle d'Atri, and

Camila Schaulsohn,

Daria Ricci

Architekturmuseum

der TUM

Although not strictly speaking a "Learning from São Paulo" exhibition, *Access for All* does have a pedagogical ambition that will become available for future use.

The accessibility of the buildings considered in this installation has been a key preoccupation for us. Not all of them have free admission or are completely open, but parts of them usually are. Part of the success of these buildings has to do with the way they are administered, their specialized staff, and the fact that they are safe places through a symbiosis between the architecture and the maintenance/security. The arguments of the installation, the larger exhibition, and the catalogue are supported with archival evidence and new architectural drawings by Guilherme Pianca and Gabriel Sepe, illustrations by Danilo Zamboni, and photographs by Ciro Miguel. The exhibition also includes a series of on-site interviews by Pedro Kok that weave together critical analyses of the case studies by local experts and some of the buildings' designers.

Just what is it that makes today's São Paulo so different, so appealing? Beyond a more complete subway system, better control of security, and other such details, what makes the city exciting today, at least in part, can be explained by the analyses of the case studies selected for this installation, and a series of other buildings of a similar nature—especially when they are understood as a network that supports life in the city, havens that make urban intensity more bearable, that favor encounters between people, and that, in the most interesting cases, empower them via sports, cultural, and educational activities.

Paulo

The Resilience of Venice

Laura Fregolent and
Paola Malanotte-Rizzoli

Ver

Venice created a civilization which lasted for one thousand years, resisted the invasions of the barbarians and the army of the Holy Roman Empire, and prevented the lagoon from becoming land. A civilization of intellectual freedom, Renaissance revival, and entrepreneurship, which became a city of incomparable beauty. Venice will survive the challenge of climate change.

1. INTRODUCTION

The overall theme of this essay is the resilience of Venice. It consists of two parts presenting different and complementary aspects of this resilience.

The first part, "Venice and Its Lagoon," focuses on the physical and morphological components of Venice's resilience. It provides a historical perspective on how the human interventions made by the Serenissima Republic changed the configuration of the lagoon on an unprecedented scale, insuring the survival of the city, its trade, and civilization against its numerous enemies. The human interventions of the twentieth century were economically driven and were meant to make the city and its region resilient for survival in a modern, industrialized world. The challenge for the future is to undertake further, major interventions to insure resilience to global warming and the danger of unprecedented sea level rise. The physical survival of the city, its millennial structure, and unique way of living are at stake.

The second part, "Venice and Its Urban Fabrics," focuses on the urban aspects of resilience, how this has evolved from the past to the present and must be reinvented for the future. It provides a perspective on the physical and social fragility of the city but also of its resilient capacity which, if properly managed, can reverse the trend that the city is witnessing.

2. VENICE AND ITS LAGOON
2.1. Human Interventions

Like all great cities which created an ancient and long-lasting civilization, the foundation of Venice is lost in legend.[1] However, the successive waves

1 Roberto Cessi, *Storia della Repubblica di Venezia* (Bologna: Giunti Martello Publisher, 1981), 824.

of barbarian invasions from eastern and central Europe into Italy with the decline of the Roman empire are well documented. Goths, Huns, and different Germanic tribes spread southward. The most devastating, massive invasion was by the Longobards in 568 CE who conquered the entire northern regions. As a result, the inhabitants of small countryside villages spread eastward and southward. Those living near the gulf of the northern Adriatic found refuge on a number of small islands, 118 in total, inside a vast lagoon—the lagoon itself being their best protection. The legend claims that the first island in which they settled was Torcello (meaning "little tower"). Among the prominent families, a *dux* was elected, which later became the Venetian *doge*. By the late 700s, the Rialto islands were permanently settled. On the island of Olivolo (now Castello) the church of San Pietro di Castello was consecrated and remained the Cathedral of Venice until the beginning of the nineteenth century. This is the beginning of the history of the Serenissima, the Most Serene Republic of Venice, as recounted by its first biographer, Deacon Giovanni.

The lagoon of Venice is a crucial part of its history. It is a dynamic environment which has never been in morphological "equilibrium" but has been continuously modified by the ancient and present-day Venetians. At the top of its splendor, in the fifteenth and sixteenth centuries, Venice was arguably the richest, most powerful state in northern Italy, with a land dominion covering the entire Veneto region, the Dalmatian coast, and many Greek islands. These dominions were coveted by many European powers. In December 1508 the League of Cambrai was formed. Under the leadership of Pope Julius II, it comprised the Holy Roman Empire, France, Spain, Hungary, the dukes of Savoy, Ferrara, and Mantua. In May 1509 the Venetian army was crushed at the famous battle of Agnadello and all land under Venice's dominion was appropriated by the League partners. The legend goes that Venice itself was saved by the lagoon from being

2 See Antonio Bondesan and Paola Furlanetto, "Artificial Fluvial Diversions in the Mainland of the Lagoon of Venice During the 16th and 17th Centuries Inferred from Historical Cartography Analysis," *Alluvial Geomorphology in Italy* 18, no. 12 (2012): 175–200.

Laura Fregolent and Paola Malanotte-Rizzoli

sacked, as the Emperor's cannon fire was unable to reach the city. But Venice was resilient: seven years later, Doge Andrea Gritti had reconquered all the land it had lost.

Here begins the first enormous modification of the lagoon system. The Venetians realized that the lagoon was undergoing an inevitable transformation into land thanks to the enormous sediment loads deposited by the rivers flowing into it. They undertook the enormous enterprise of changing the course of the rivers, moving their estuaries outside the lagoon in successive phases. During the sixteenth and seventeenth centuries the courses of the Brenta, Bacchiglione, Adige, Marengo, Sile, and Piave rivers were diverted, some to the south, some to the north of the lagoon.[2] But the lagoon was preserved and it protected Venice until the last, fatal invasion by Napoleon in 1797.

After this massive alteration of the lagoon's morphology, its sedimentary budget became negative. And thanks to other human-made modifications made in the twentieth century, today the lagoon is in a state of erosion. The salt marshes are disappearing: in the last seventy years or so, their coverage has decreased from 25% to 8% of its surface. The sediment loss at sea is about 700,000 m3/year. The lagoon is becoming a marine environment. Its natural habitat of shellfish, clams, crabs, small fish, and local birds is disappearing. Marshes are presently being artificially reconstructed to restore the lagoon's natural ecosystem.

Fig. 1 shows the major human interventions of the twentieth century. Among them, a significant increase in the erosive processes was produced by digging a deep "oil" channel in the 1970s. Starting from the Malamocco inlet, built in the nineteenth century, the channel allows the passage of oil containers so they may reach the industrial docks of Porto Marghera. The inlet depth was increased from about 5 meters to the current 15 meters, which is also the depth of the channel. Consequently, the velocity of the tide flushing Venice twice a day is much greater, erosive processes along the channel are much more intense, and the export of sediments out of the lagoon has considerably increased, as discussed above.

Fig. 1—Modifications of
the Venice lagoon in the
twentieth century.

Fig. 2—Loss of the
ground elevation (cm)
with respect to the 1908
mean sea level.

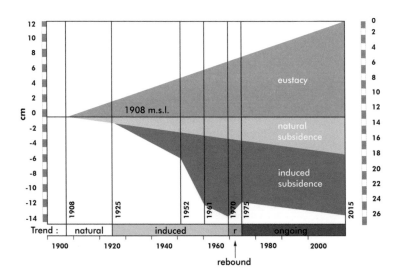

Laura Fregolent and Paola Malanotte-Rizzoli

The second major human-made modifications of the lagoon started in the 1920s, when a considerable portion of the northwestern part of the lagoon was transformed into land to create the industrial zone of Marghera, marked with a red circle in Fig. 1. The number of workers employed rose to about 40,000 in the 1970s. On the positive side, the industrial development produced an economic boost for the region. On the negative side, though, it irreversibly altered the nature of the sedimentary bottom of the entire lagoon and nearby mainland. This bottom is constituted by a series of alternating aquifers and aquitards. The aquifers are sedimentary layers very rich in water, and are interlaced with the aquitards, which are impermeable to water. The Marghera industries exploited the aquifers by pumping so much water out of them that a vast majority collapsed. During the previous centuries, the natural subsidence of the lagoon was due to the compacting of sediments with a rate estimated at 0.5 mm/year.[3] The human-induced subsidence due to the collapsing of aquifers resulted in a cumulative twelve centimeters of subsidence from 1925 to 1970.

The phenomenon of eusthatism must also be mentioned. Eusthatism is the long-term sea level rise in response to climate change. The global rise throughout the twentieth century was of 1.7 mm/year in the twentieth century; it has increased to 3.2 mm/year in the last two decades. Fig. 2 summarizes the combined effects of total subsidence and eusthatism.[4] It shows the loss of ground elevation in centimeters with respect to the 1908 mean sea level. The human-induced subsidence, in red, shows the dramatic increase between 1925 and 1970. In 1970 a law was approved to prevent any further exploitation of the underground aquifers. A short period of rebound followed, due to a slight repressurization of the aquifers. Combined with the eusthatic sea level rise, the cumulative result was a twenty-six centimeter loss of ground elevation from 1908 to now. In other words, Venice and its lagoon are presently twenty-six centimeters lower than they were in 1908.

3 See Paolo Gatto and Laura Carbognin, "The Lagoon of Venice: Natural Environment Trend and Man-Induced Modification," *Hydrological Science Journal* 24, no. 4 (1981): 375–391.

4 Adapted from Fabio Trincardi, Andrea Barbanti, Mauro Bastianini, Alvise Benetazzo, Luigi Cavaleri, Jacopo Chiggiato, Alvise Papa, Angela Pomaro, Mauro Sclavo, Luigi Tosi, and Georg Umgiesser, "The 1966 Flooding of Venice," *Oceanography* 29, no. 4 (2016): 178–186.

ce

This twenty-six centimeter loss of ground elevation has had dire consequences for the lagoon system. The phenomenon of recurrent floods (*acqua alta*) is by now well-known all over the world. Contrary to popular belief, it is not due to the astronomical tide. Dominated by the semidiurnal tide, the astronomical tide is extremely small in the Mediterranean Sea, rising to about five centimeters, even though it reaches its maximum excursion of about fifty centimeters on average in the northern Adriatic because of its very shallow depth. The floods are due to the storm surge—also called the meteorological tide—of the Adriatic Sea itself. Under the meteorological conditions of the sirocco wind, which blows from the southeast all along the Adriatic major axis, water is piled up at its northern extremity, i.e., Venice and its lagoon. Hence the floods. Fig. 3 shows the consequence of the ground level lowering. The blue line shows the ground reference level of 1908. The red line shows the relative ground level resulting from the human-induced subsidence from 1925 to 1970 and the sea level rise. The vertical, thin lines represent the peaks of high water from 1910 to 2019. Storm surges 110 cm in height would not have flooded the lagoon and the city in 1908. A hundred centimeter level is considered as the threshold for danger in the city. Presently at ninety centimeters, San Marco Square is completely submerged. During the storm surge of November 4, 1966 and the recent, multiple surges of November 2019, 90% of the city was under water.

2.2. The Challenge of Climate Change

Climate change is unequivocal. On a global scale, the data over the last one hundred years show dramatic changes in global properties, from the unprecedented increase in global average temperature, to the increasing rate of global sea level rise, to the frequency of extreme events. The crucial problem is predicting what will happen in the future under global warming scenarios. The 2013 AR5 Report of the Intergovernmental Panel for Climate Change established worldwide accepted scenarios for the changes expected through the end of this century.[5]

5   The Intergovernmental Panel on Climate Change (IPCC), *Fifth Assessment Report* (Cambridge, UK: Cambridge University Press, 2013), 1552.

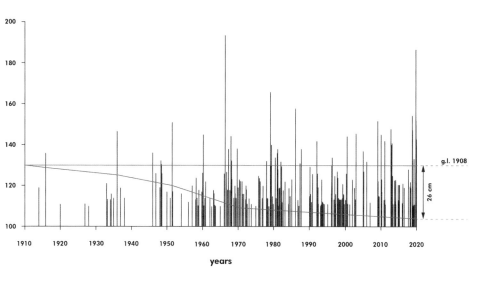

Fig. 3 – High water events (vertical lines) in Venice since 1910. The blue line represents the ground reference level (ge) of 1908. The red line shows relative ground level loss in time resulting from the sinking of Venice rising sea level.

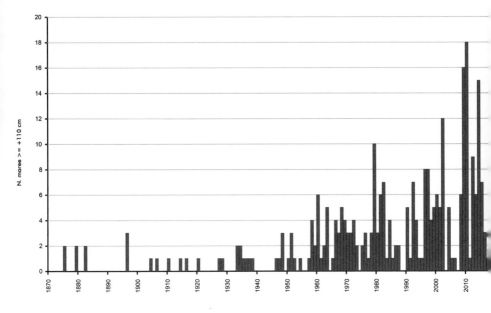

Coastal cities and shallow regions of the world are among the cities that will suffer the most. First and foremost, is Venice and its lagoon. While mitigation and adaptation measures are imperative to ensuring the habitability of the city and of the islands, much greater measures must be envisioned for their actual survival.

The available data unequivocally show this change. Tidal gauge records for Venice go back to the late nineteenth century. The tidal gauge at Punta della Salute is taken as the reference point for sea level elevation. As previously mentioned, 110 cm above mean sea level is considered the threshold at which a considerable part of the city is submerged. Fig. 4 shows the time evolution of the sea level data through the end of 2019. The interannual variability of the record is great. Many years of the last decades

Fig. 4—Yearly distribution of high tides >= +110 cm recorded in Venice, from 1875 to 2019.

Laura Fregolent and Paola Malanotte-Rizzoli

Ver

experienced one or two high waters exceeding 110 cm, 2017 being the latest example. However, since 1970, their number has increased exponentially. The last extreme events in Fig. 1 are those of November 2019.

As previously discussed, the sea level rise in the lagoon is produced by the storm surge of the Adriatic Sea under the sirocco wind blowing from the southeast along its axis. The semidiurnal astronomical tide has an average excursion around mean sea level from about -10 cm to about 40 cm. There are, however, extreme situations: the so-called spring tides, occurring when the sun and moon are both in line with the Earth. In this case the tidal range can increase from about -25 cm to about 75 cm. The linear superposition of the storm surge sea level rise and the astronomical tide produce the resulting sea level elevation. Of crucial importance is the relative phase of the two contributions, the worst scenario being when they are in phase.

The extreme meteorological condition responsible for the sirocco wind is a "megacane," i.e., a Mediterranean cyclone similar to the hurricanes of the northern Atlantic Ocean. A megacane can reach hundreds of kilometers in diameter and is centered mostly on the sea. The frequent occurrence of high waters in October and November is because these months constitute the sea's "summer." Ocean waters warm up and cool down much more slowly than the atmosphere. The megacane lives and grows in intensity by extracting heat (energy) from the warm sea. The megacane of 1966 covered the entire Italian Peninsula and was responsible for the destruction of Venice and Florence.

According to the last IPCC Special Report on global warming of September 2018, in the last five decades human activities have caused about 1°C of temperature increase above preindustrial levels. Global warming is likely to reach 1.5°C between 2030 and 2050 if it continues to increase at the present rate. Even though these estimates are global averages, and not regional ones, their implications for the increase of extreme events are clear. Specifically for the Adriatic Sea and Venice, increased ocean and air temperatures imply an

ce

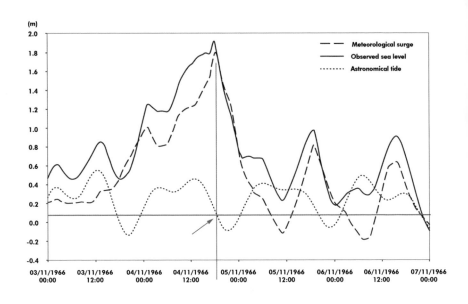

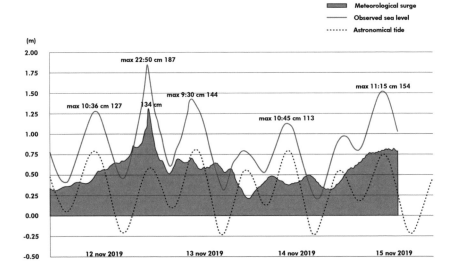

Laura Fregolent and Paola Malanotte-Rizzoli

increase in the strength of cyclones and of related winds. The effect of the global warming which has occurred over the last fifty years, from 1966 to 2019, is evident in the comparison of the famous "*acqua granda*" of 1966 and the successive sea level extremes of November 2019.

Fig. 5 shows the evolution of the meteorological surge, the astronomical tide, and the resulting sea level for 1966, characterized by one single extreme event of 194 cm. On that occasion, the astronomical tide had its normal range of about 40 cm. Furthermore, the 1966 "*acqua granda*" was a "lucky" event. As it is clear in Fig. 5, the vertical red line centered at the peak of the meteorological tide was out of phase with the astronomical tide. This latter tide, at the same moment, had zero amplitude. Had the surge occurred a few hours earlier, the sea level rise would have reached the height of 234 cm (194 + 40 cm).

This unfortunately was not the case for November 2019. Fig. 6 shows the successive five extreme high waters in the period from November 12 to 15. First, the astronomical tide was a spring one, reaching extreme heights of 55–75 cm. Even though the strongest meteorological surge of November 12 was only of 134 cm, it was exactly in phase with the spring tide. The combined effects of the two gave a sea level rise of 187 cm. Because of this "phase locking," there were five successive high peaks in sea level, as Fig. 6 shows. Finally, the winds in the November 2019 case were much stronger than in 1966, causing extreme and much greater destructions than in 1966.

Figs. 4 and 6 do not bode well for future floods. The expected global increase of 1.5°C by 2050 will dramatically increase the frequency of extreme meteorological cyclones and attendant extreme floods. Extreme measures must urgently be taken to prevent their consequences on Venice and its lagoon. Let us hope that today's Venetians and Italians will be not only capable but especially willing to take these measures and face the final challenge of global warming. The ancient Venetians surely were.

Fig. 5 — Time history of the flood of 4 November 1966 in Venice.

Fig. 6 — Time history of the flood of 12–15 November 2019.

ce

3. VENICE AND ITS URBAN FABRIC
3.1. Venice Between Past and Future

The amphibious city of Venice owes its particular urban form to the centuries-old coexistence and interaction between water, land, and the artifacts of humans. From the very beginning, humans have diverted rivers; dug canals; and reclaimed, swamped, buried, or improved parts of the lagoon terrain in order to defend the city from invasions and maintain the condition and character of the commercial city.

Until the eighteenth century, that is, until the fall of the Republic, this system of land and water had, for ten centuries, been skillfully maintained, and a balance was found between the lagoon and the city by a unitary government guaranteed by the Serenissima Republic of Venice. It is a success story in environmental governance that had its origins in the action of the stern but visionary government of the Republic; in the daily, centuries-old effort to control private and individual interests and their adaptation to the superior public good with regard to the water and the city; in the ability to create a balance between economic freedom and the entrepreneurial initiative of citizens, with the constraints imposed by collective resources.[6]

The fall of the Venetian Republic in 1797 marked a profound break in the city and lagoon administration, but above all a break in the fragile relationship between humans and nature.[7] The lagoon moved towards transformations that complied with modernity, responding to the needs of a "new" economy that over time progressively required, for example, deeper channels suitable for the transit of increasingly large and spacious ships, more solid land margins, and larger artificial islands.

In modern times, Venice's spice and fabric cargoes of the past have been overtaken by chemistry and the transport of petroleum and refined products for the industrial area of Porto Marghera, which was built at the beginning of the twentieth century on the edge of the lagoon overlooking the historic city.

6 See Pietro Bevilaqua, *Venezia e le sue acque* (Rome: Donzelli, 1998).

7 See Edoardo Salzano, *La laguna di Venezia* (Venice: Corte del Fontego, 2011).

8 See Bruno Anastasia and Giancarlo Corò, *I distretti industriali in Veneto* (Portogruaro, Italy: Ediciclo, 1993).

9 See the monographic issue on Venice, Aa. Vv., *Urbanistica* 59–60 (January 1972).

10 See Leonardo Ciacci, *Abitare a Venezia negli anni '80* (Milan: A. Giuffrè, 1981).

11 Francesco Indovina, "Venezia, opera d'arte deperibile," *L'illustrazione italiana* 94 (1997): 20–29 and Isabella Scaramuzzi, "Turismo: un'industria pesante," in *1950–2000: L'Italia è cambiata*, eds. Francesco Indovina, Laura Fregolent, Michelangelo Savino, 235–250 (Milan: FrancoAngeli, 2000).

Laura Fregolent and Paola Malanotte-Rizzoli

In 1979 a peak of 40,000 employees was reached, but at the beginning of the 1970s the industrial area, and with it the whole industrial model, entered a period of crisis, from which a new, important model developed, based on small- and medium-sized enterprises, which gave rise to a powerful boom in the economy of the region in the '80s and '90s.[8]

However, modern Venice is also a fragile city, which is progressively losing inhabitants: from 174,808 residents in the historic city center in 1951, the population has plummeted to 52,143 in 2019. An "exodus" saw more than 120,000 people leave the island city for the mainland in search of larger houses at lower prices, better services, and, more generally, different living and cohabitation conditions.

The reasons for such a decrease in population starting in 1951 are manifold: First, the building stocks are very run-down dwellings. In addition, the increase in commuting, and the ensuing workers' demand to be nearer to their workplaces on the mainland, also carries significant weight. The selection is based mainly on income, that is, those who leave the island city typically live in rented accommodations, on the ground floor or in buildings which require huge restoration expenditure.[9]

To these economic conditions major and catastrophic events for the island city are added—catastrophes such as the high water in 1966 and 1979, which contributed towards further exacerbating the exodus phenomenon from the historic city center, even if the "great migration" had already occurred (Fig. 7). This radically changed the social structure of the city and transformed Venice into a middle-class clerical town with heavy public investment in maintenance work and conservation of historic and monumental heritage.[10]

Those who continue to live in Venice are faced with the deterioration of their houses, the high costs of maintenance, and more recently, with the discomfort caused by the masses of tourists who invade the city and public transport systems and rob the residential market of housing. The exodus has depopulated the city and left behind an aging population, while tourism—constantly on the rise—has become the most important economic sector, changing the face of Venice.[11]

3.2. Urban Form, Activities, and Functions of the Present

The urban fabric of Venice is very compact and homogeneous, the result of a morphological evolution and progressive, intensive building, which established that famous, consolidated urban form of the city. *Campi* (squares), *campielli* (smaller squares), *corti* (courtyards), *salizade* (broad paved paths), *fondamenta* (paved river and canal paths) and *rio terà* (covered-over waterways) compose public open spaces, which have a special function and use in Venice, but the water, too, is an immense public space, experienced both in the urban part of the city and in the lagoon (Fig. 8).

Regarding public space, there are various new economic activities today, specifically those connected to the dynamics of tourism with still a few remnants of traditional trades and crafts. Thus we have witnessed, in the course of the last decades, a progressive banalization of the Venetian urban landscape due to the difficulty of maintaining traditional activities to respond to the demand of an ever-increasing number of non-resident users. This, in turn, has created a niche for a tiny, often trivial and standardized trade, and, at the same time, a luxury trade linked to the large labels and multinationals of this sector, which have colonized the heart of city and brought Venice and its unique urban structure in line with the other mass tourist cities.

Trade is the "litmus test" of the transformations that have taken place. If we take a look at the data of licenses issued by the Municipality of Venice, we become aware of a progressive increase in the number of licenses issued in the food and catering sector (restaurants, snack bars, cafés, pizzerias). From 2015 to 2019, it climbed from 2,316 to 2,506 respectively (increasing by 8%) but trade in general (local shops, medium-sized sales businesses, large sales structures and shopping centers) also rose from 7,260 in 2015 to 8,494 in 2019 (increasing by 17%).

There is, therefore, a polarization in certain sectors confirmed by analysis conducted in the field (Fig. 9), which highlights the presence of shops with a principal tourist "vocation" along the main tourist routes, the replacement of a more

Fig. 7—Population trend.

Fig. 8—Urban and lagoon fabric, Venice.

Laura Fregolent and Paola Malanotte-Rizzoli

Ver

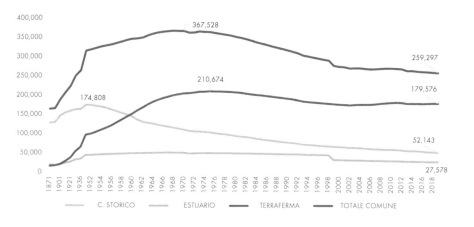

——— C. STORICO	——— ESTUARIO	——— TERRAFERMA	——— TOTALE COMUNE

- neighborhood shops
- food
- souvenir
- clothings and luxury goods
- other

- Residential entrance
- Hotel, B&B
- Shops
- Other

0   1,25   2,5   5 Kilometers

N

Laura Fregolent and Paola Malanotte-Rizzoli

Ver

traditional commercial structure, and the transformation of the ways and forms of selling the same food products, which are increasingly oriented towards transit flows with fast food and takeaway offers. This trend has ended up infecting even the traditional activities of the street market where, for some time now, packaged products, fresh or otherwise, coexist with fresh goods for the exclusive use of the passing buyer.

All this obviously needs to be viewed within a more extensive international framework, in which the processes of globalization are evidently manifested by the radical trans-formations which trade is subject to—an intensive, potentially unstoppable phenomena, and, in the case of Venice, with an even more marked impact due to its unique urban structure and the intensity which the tourist phenomenon has been shown to possess.[12]

But apart from the type of activity and its prevailing user, that which we wish to highlight is the use of the ground floors, not only for productive, commercial or craft activities but also for residential use, often with receptive purposes and therefore destined for tourism (Fig. 10).

3.3. Rethinking the Future

Despite the outline of a "fragilized" Venice regarding its residential component, a city subject to an increase in the number and intensity of high water occurrences (Fig. 11), Venice is still a residential city: it is a city of people who live and spend most of their time there; of workers who live elsewhere but operate there; of craftsmen and retailers who hold out with their shops and workshops full of everyday products; of noisy children who draw landscapes and fantasy animals with colored chalks on the *masegni* (massive paving stones) in the city squares; of everyday conversations exchanged on bridges between shopping bags and barrows loaded with wares to be delivered. It is a continuous battle between the slow tempo of the city and the fast beat imposed by modernity. And for those who love this city,

12 See Sharon Zukin, Philip Kasinitz, and Chen Xiangming, eds. *Global Cities, Local Streets: Everyday Diversity from New York to Shanghai* (New York: Routledge, 2016).

Fig. 9—Commercial activities, Venice, 2019.

Fig. 10—Ground floor functions, Venice, 2019.

ce

it is this dimension that they appreciate and would protect from the tidal wave of tourists.

At this point a reflection must be made about the health crisis we are currently experiencing. The COVID-19 virus is putting a severe strain on the world and health care systems of the various countries involved. Its effects on the urban fabric, as well as on the economy, are already partly visible: the city is empty, public space is deserted, tourists have disappeared, shops are closed, except those which sell food and medicine. An unimaginable city, at least up until the end of February 2020.

This new condition that we have to deal with will significantly change usage and functions for a period not yet calculable. The saying, "It will all go back to what it was before" does not seem to be an expendable slogan at present.

It is here, starting with a condition of uncertainty, but also of profound change, that we must rethink our existence together, our places of cohabitation and life spaces, which will possibly be used more by residents than transit tourists.

This will mean rethinking our daily lives and the way we live, perhaps repopulating the city if we can physically take back its spaces, and giving new spaces to activities and economies capable of strengthening the craftmanship, commercial, and cultural sectors—namely those that economically and socially existent. This will mean reaffirming that "resilient" capacity which Venice has had over the centuries, its strength to resist but also to adapt and keep its nature intact whilst changing.

Venice must keep alive its vocation as a city of history and culture; it has to turn to the past to span a thread of continuity to the present and the future.

PROJECT CREDITS

Laura Fregolent and Paola

Malanotte-Rizzoli with

Renato Gibin, Valerio

Volpe, Alessandra Longo,

Dalila Quartucci, Matteo

Basso, Elena Zambardi,

Paolo De Benedictis,

Studio De Benedictis

University Iuav of Venice,

Massachusetts Institute of

Technology

Laura Fregolent and Paola Malanotte-Rizzoli

Ver

Fig. 11—High water in San Marco square, Venice.

BIOGRAPHIES

ADDIS ABABA
Marc Angélil
Marc Angélil is a practicing architect at *agps architecture*, with ateliers in Los Angeles and Zurich. He holds the 2021 Kenzo Tange Visiting Professorship at Harvard University and is professor emeritus from ETH Zurich, conducting research on socio-spatial developments of metropolitan regions worldwide. His most recent publication *Mirroring Effects: Tales of Territory* was written in collaboration with Cary Siress.

Cary Siress
Cary Siress is an architect and Senior Researcher in Territorial Organization at ETH Zurich. His research pertains to global urbanization processes and how human and material realms become entangled under various political-economic agendas.

AL AZRAQ CAMP
Azra Akšamija
Azra Akšamija (PhD) is an artist and architectural historian, Director of the Future Heritage Lab (FHL), and Associate Professor in the Program in Art, Culture and Technology at the School of Architecture + Planning at MIT. Her work explores how social life is affected by cultural bias and by the deterioration and destruction of cultural infrastructures within the context of conflict, migration, and displacement.

Melina Philippou
Melina Philippou is an architect, urbanist, and researcher. She is the Program Director of the Future Heritage Lab (FHL) at MIT. Her work explores the agency of spatial practices in the context of forced displacement.

BEIRUT
Sandra Frem
Sandra Frem is a lecturer at the American University of Beirut and the Lebanese American University, and co-founder of platau | platform for architecture and urbanism. Working between academic research and practice, her work probes the overlays of architecture, landscape, and practices of the urban environment to open up speculations on their interdependence. She holds an SMArchS in Urbanism from MIT and a DES in Architecture from the Lebanese University.

Boulos Douaihy
Boulos Douaihy is an architect, geographer, activist, and lecturer at the Lebanese American University. He is the founding principal of platau | platform for architecture and urbanism, a design research practice dedicated to expand the agency of architecture at multiple scales, from material to territory. He holds a DES in Architecture from the Lebanese University and a M.A. in "Environment et Aménagement du Territoire" from Université St Joseph.

HONG KONG

Merve Bedir

Merve Bedir is an architect, focusing on design as a research-based, collective, transscalar, and beyond disciplinary act. She is an adjunct assistant professor in Hong Kong University, Faculty of Architecture.

Sampson Wong

Sampson Wong is an academic, artist, and independent curator, working on the topics of contemporary urbanism, space and geography, art and the public, cultural resistance and hope. He takes care of the Umbrella Movement Visual Archive, and he is a member of the Add Oil team.

INDIA

Rahul Mehrotra

Rahul Mehrotra is a practicing architect, urban designer, and educator. He works in Mumbai and Boston, and teaches at the Graduate School of Design at Harvard University where he is professor of urban design and planning. His practice, RMA Architects, founded in 1990, has executed a range of projects, mainly in India. Mehrotra has written, co-authored, and edited a vast repertoire of books on Mumbai, its urban history, historic buildings, public spaces, and planning processes.

Sourav Kumar Biswas

Sourav Kumar Biswas is a landscape planner and spatial analyst with design and planning experience in Afghanistan, China, India, and the US. He is the Practice Area Lead for Urban and Landscape Planning at Geoadaptive in Boston. He has written books on urban informality, nature-based solutions, and co-authored a forthcoming book on India's emergent urbanization patterns.

MEXICO/EGYPT/NIGERIA

Kent Larson

Kent Larson directs the City Science group at the MIT Media Lab. His research focuses on developing urban interventions that enable more entrepreneurial, livable, and resilient communities. To that end, his projects include advanced simulation and augmented reality for urban design, transformable micro-housing for millennials, mobility-on-demand systems that create alternatives to private automobiles, and Urban Living Lab deployments via a connected network of international collaborators.

Gabriela Bílá Advincula

Gabriela (Gabi) Bílá Advincula is a graduate researcher at the MIT Media Lab, architect, multimedia designer, and artist. Gabi explores the contemporary city as raw material, combining new media and tangible interfaces to reimagine our future. Her past exhibitions include *Teleport City and the New Guide to Brasilia* in addition to a City Science collaboration at the Cooper Hewitt Museum.

Luis Alonso

Luis Alonso is a research scientist and the principal Investigator of the City Science Lab at Andorra. He has a PhD in architecture, and he coordinates several projects in the City Science Network. His research focus includes: urban indicators, big data analysis, urban planning, architectural robotics, building design and construction, smart materials, energy simulation, building efficiency, sustainability, and other emerging technologies.

Maitane Iruretagoyena

Maitane Iruretagoyena is a technical associate and researcher working on several projects on new technologies to create innovative places where people live and work. Maitane studied Building Engineering and Technical Architecture and she has a master's degree in Sustainable Construction and Energy Efficiency from the University of the Basque Country in San Sebastian, Spain.

Guadalupe Babio

Guadalupe Babio is a graduate researcher at the MIT Media Lab with a high-level understanding of emerging technologies. Her research is focused on bridging the interface between urban planning, architecture, and new technologies to improve the quality of life in cities. Guadalupe graduated from the School of Architecture of Madrid, ETSAM, and participated in student exchanges programs at Tongji University in China and Technion University in Israel.

Thomas Sanchez Lengeling

Thomas Sanchez Lengeling is a research scientist, artist, and engineer interested in creating experiences that allow people to change their perspective by blending perceptual experiences with digital information. His research is at the intersection of science, art, and technology. He works in mobility, artificial intelligence, wearable technology, immersive experiences, music, and educational outreach.

Holger Prang

Holger Prang is a research associate in the City Science Lab at HafenCity University in Hamburg, Germany. He is part of the CityScope team involved in the development of data-driven negotiation themes and knowledge management to support participation and collaboration throughout disciplines. His PhD research focuses on semantic data analytics and knowledge-mapping in spatial and social phenomena.

Nicolas Ayoub
Nicolas Ayoub is a product designer and strategist. Previously, he was a visiting researcher in the City Science group at at the MIT Media Lab. Nicolas has a master's degree in Design and Technology from Harvard University. He works at the nexus of society, technology, and design, and he has worked with design studios and startups in Europe, Asia, and the United States.

Margaret Church
Margaret Church is responsible for research coordination, events, and workshops at the MIT Media Lab. She also helps with communications and proposals for the City Science Network, a group of international cities striving to create more livable and equitable communities. She co-organizes the annual City Science Summit with collaborators from the home institutions.

NEW YORK—
COLUMBIA UNIVERSITY
GRADUATE SCHOOL OF
ARCHITECTURE, PLANNING AND
PRESERVATION (GSAPP)
The Housing Lab
The GSAPP Housing Lab gathers leaders across planning, design, and development to innovate for action at the intersection of housing and climate change. Through interdisciplinary partnerships in research, pedagogy, and practice, the lab deploys methods that aim to shift the rules of existing systems of housing toward resilience, inclusion, and access.

Daisy Ames
Daisy Ames is an Adjunct Assistant Professor at Columbia University GSAPP, where she teaches architecture studios and also serves as the architecture faculty of the GSAPP Housing Lab. Ames is the founding principal of Studio Ames, an architectural design studio based in New York City. She holds a BA from Brown University and an M.Arch I from Yale School of Architecture.

Adam Snow Frampton
Adam Snow Frampton, AIA is the Principal of Only If, a New York-based design practice for architecture and urbanism that he founded in 2013. He also teaches at Columbia University GSAPP and co-authored *Cities Without Ground: A Hong Kong Guidebook* (2012). He previously worked for seven years as an Associate at OMA and holds an M.Arch from Princeton University.

Bernadette Baird-Zars
Bernadette Baird-Zars is the IDC fellow at the GSAPP Housing Lab and a PhD candidate in urban planning at Columbia University. As a partner at Alarife Urban

Associates, she leads projects on land use and housing innovation. Recent publications include *Zoning: a Guide for 21st Century Planning* (Routledge, 2020) and articles on planning practices in JPER (2018) and MELG (2019).

NEW YORK—
IRWIN S. CHANIN SCHOOL OF ARCHITECTURE, COOPER UNION

Nora Akawi
Nora Akawi is Assistant Professor of Architecture at The Cooper Union. Previously, Nora taught at Columbia University, where she was Director of Studio-X Amman. She co-edited the book *Architecture and Representation: The Arab City* (2016). Selected exhibitions include *Friday Sermon* (16th International Architecture Exhibition, Venice Biennale, 2018), and *This Land's Unknown* (Biennale d'Architecture, Orléans, 2019).

Hayley Eber
Hayley Eber is an architect and educator. She is currently the Assistant Dean at The Cooper Union and the Principal of Studio Eber, an award-winning New York-based practice for architecture and design. She has taught at Princeton University and Columbia University GSAPP, and her work has been published in *Domus*, *Praxis*, *DETAIL*, and *Pidgin*, amongst others.

Lydia Kallipoliti
Lydia Kallipoliti (PhD) is an architect, engineer, theorist, curator, and educator, with degrees from Princeton University and MIT. She is currently an Assistant Professor at The Cooper Union, and previously taught at Rensselaer Polytechnic Institute where she directed the MS Program, Syracuse University, and Columbia University. Her work has been exhibited internationally including the Oslo Triennale, the London Design Museum, the Disseny Hub Barcelona, the Istanbul Biennal, the Shenzen Biennale, and the Storefront for Art and Architecture. She is the author of the award-winning book, *The Architecture of Closed Worlds* (Lars Muller, 2018).

Lauren Kogod
Lauren Kogod is an architect and architectural historian with essays published in *Assemblage*, *A+U*, *Quaderns*, *AD Monograph: Enric Miralles*, *Harvard Design Magazine*, *Grey Room*, and *Architecture and Capitalism: 1845 to the Present* (Routledge, 2014). She has taught at The Cooper Union, Yale University, and Barnard College and Columbia University, among other schools.

Ife Vanable
Ife Vanable is an architect, theorist, and historian who holds degrees in architecture from Cornell University and

235

Princeton University. Ife is founder and leader of i/van/able, a Visiting Professor at the Irwin S. Chanin School of Architecture of The Cooper Union, and a PhD candidate in architectural history and theory at Columbia University GSAPP.

PRISHTINA
Bekim Ramku
Bekim Ramku, architect and urbanist, is the founding director of the Kosovo Architecture Foundation (est. 2012) and the Kosovo Architecture Festival; he manages his Prishtina-based practice OUD+Architects. Ramku served as a technical reviewer and a coordinator to the Aga Khan Award for Architecture in 2016 and 2019. He studied at the University of Prishtina, the AA School of Architecture, and MIT.

RIO DE JANEIRO
Sérgio Burgi
Sérgio Burgi heads the photography department of the Moreira Salles Institute in Rio de Janeiro, Brazil's leading institution dedicated to the conservation and preservation of photographic collections. Burgi recently curated the exhibition, *Marc Ferrez—Território e Imagem* (2019).

Farès el-Dahdah
Farès el-Dahdah is Professor of the Humanities and Director of the Humanities Research Center at Rice University. El-Dahdah's research focuses on developing geodatabases that describe cities and sites over time, as they existed and as they have come to be imagined and with Alida C. Metcalf and Axis Maps, he developed the cartographic platform *imagineRio*.

Alida C. Metcalf
Alida C. Metcalf is Harris Masterson, Jr. Professor of History at Rice University in Houston, USA. Metcalf is the author of *The Return of Hans Staden: A Go-between in the Atlantic World* (2012) with Eve M. Duffy and *Mapping an Atlantic World circa 1500* (2020). With Farès el-Dahdah and Axis Maps, she developed the cartographic platform *imagineRio*.

David Heyman
David Heyman is an interactive cartographer and managing director of Axis Maps, a cartographic design studio specializing in bringing the traditions of cartography to interactive media. With partners Andy Woodruff and Ben Sheesley, Axis Maps designs and builds interactive maps and data visualizations that communicate geographic phenomena for clients in diverse fields ranging from spatial history to healthcare to the environment.

SÃO PAULO

Daniel Talesnik

Daniel Talesnik is Assistant Professor of the History of Architecture and Curatorial Practice and Curator at the Architekturmuseum der TUM. He is a trained architect from the Universidad Católica de Chile and was awarded a PhD in History and Theory of Architecture by Columbia University. He specializes in modern and contemporary architecture and urbanism, with a particular focus on architectural pedagogy and relationships between architecture and political ideologies.

VENICE

Laura Fregolent

Laura Fregolent, architect, is Full Professor of Urban Planning at the University Iuav of Venice. Her research focuses on urban sprawl and interactions with policy and planning tools, urban transformations and social dynamics, the relationship between processes of growth, and morphological and socio-economic transformations. In the last years her research case study has been the city of Venice.

Paola Malanotte-Rizzoli

Paola Malanotte-Rizzoli joined MIT in 1981. She is Professor of Physical Oceanography and Climate. She is the author and co-author of 147 scientific refereed publications in international journals and of 14 refereed books. She has worked since the early 1970s on the problems affecting Venice and its lagoon.

IMAGE CREDITS

ADDIS ABABA
pages 12–13
Photo: Marta H. Wisniewska
pages 16–17
Photo: Mulugeta Ayene, AFP
pages 20–21
Getty Images and AFP,
Photo: Alexander Joe
page 22
(top) Courtesy Mezzedimi Archive;
(bottom) CGTN Africa

AL AZRAQ CAMP
pages 28–31, 36–41, 43–44
All photos: Future Heritage Lab,
School of Architecture + Planning,
Massachusettes Institute of
Technology, 2016

BEIRUT
pages 48–51, 56–58, 65 (bottom)
All photos: © Wissam Chaaya
page 55
BePublic Lab,
American University of Beirut
page 61
Louay Kabalan
page 65
(top) Oscar Asly
page 66
(top) © Beirut Urban Lab/
Ahmad Gharbieh
(bottom) © Sandra Frem
page 67 (top), 68–69
© Carla Aramouny

HONG KONG
pages 74–75, 78–81, 84–89,
92–93, 96–99
All photos: Tsang Tsz Yeung, *Language
of the Unheard* series, 2019

INDIA
pages 105–106, 109–110, 113
Census of India 2011, MLInfo Map
page 116
Uchida, H. and Nelson, A. 2010.
"Agglomeration Index: Towards a
New Measure of Urban Concentration."
Working Paper 2010/29, United Nations
University-World Institute for
Development Economics Research
(UNU-WIDER): Helsinki, Finland.
page 121
NASA Earth Observatory images by
Joshua Stevens, using Suomi NPP VIIRS
data from Miguel Román, NASA GSFC
pages 122–123
Global Administrative Areas, 2012,
GADM database of Global
Administrative Areas, version 2.0.
www.gadm.org; Global Runoff Data
Centre, 2007, Major River Basins of
the World/Global Runoff Data Centre,
Koblenz, Germany: Federal Institute
of Hydrology (BfG)

MEXICO/EGYPT/NIGERIA
pages 126, 129–130, 135–137
All photos: MIT City Science Group,
MIT Media Lab

NEW YORK–GSAPP
pages 143–144, 147–148
All images: The Housing Lab,
Graduate School of Architecture,
Planning and Preservation,
Columbia University

NEW YORK–COOPER UNION
pages 152–153, 155–156
All images: The Irwin S. Chanin
School Architecture at the
Cooper Union

PRISHTINA
pages 158–159
Ibai Rigby
page 162
Kosovo Archives
pages 167–170
All photos: Bekim Ramku

RIO DE JANEIRO
pages 172–173
George Leuzinger,
Instituto Moreira Salles
page 175
Woodson Research Center
Special Collections & Archives,
Rice University
pages 176–177
Fundação Biblioteca Nacional
page 178, 181 (top)
Marc Ferrez, Instituto
Moreira Salles
page 181 (bottom), 182–183
Augusto Malta,
Instituto Moreira Salles
page 184
Marcel Gautherot,
Instituto Moreira Salles
pages 186–189
Robert Polidori,
Instituto Moreira Salles

SÃO PAULO
pages 190–191, 198–199, 204–205
All photos: Ciro Miguel, 2019
page 193, 196, 203
Drawings: Guilherme Pianca,
Gabriel Sepe et al., 2019
pages 194–195, 200–201, 206–207
Drawings: Danilo Zamboni, 2019

VENICE
pages 214
(top) Consorzio Venezia Nuova
(bottom) Updated from Trincardi et al., 2015
page 217, 220
Updated from Trincardi et al., 2016
page 218, 225 (top)
Comune di Venezia, Centro previsioni
e segnalazioni maree
page 225 (bottom)
Ministero delle Infrastrutture e dei
Trasporti, Provveditorato Interregionale
per le Opere Pubbliche del Veneto,
Trentino Alto Adige, Friuli Venezia Giulia
page 226
(top) Elaboration of Renato Gibin, Laboratory
Cartografia e GIS, Iuav, https://iuav-labgis.
maps.arcgis.com/apps/MapJournal/index.
html?appid=c80b12379b7c4c119fed69d
2ad3845f3# Cartografia e GIS, Iuav,
https://iuav-labgis.maps.arcgis.com/apps
/MapJournal/index.html?appid=c80b12379
b7c4c119fed69d2ad3845f3#
(bottom) Elaboration of Renato Gibin,
Laboratory Cartografia e GIS, Iuav,
https://iuav-labgis.maps.arcgis.com/apps
/MapJournal/index.html?appid=c80b12379
b7c4c119fed69d2ad3845f3#
pages 228–229
Photo: G. Marcoaldi, Ministero delle
Infrastrutture e dei Trasporti,
Provveditorato Interregionale per le
Opere Pubbliche del Veneto, Trentino
Alto Adige, Friuli Venezia Giulia

239

Editors
Hashim Sarkis and Ala Tannir

Authors
Marc Angélil and Cary Siress;
Nora Akawi, Hayley Eber, Lydia
Kallipoliti, Lauren Kogod, and
Ife Vanable (The Irwin S. Chanin School
of Architecture at the Cooper Union);
Azra Akšamija and Melina Philippou
(MIT Future Heritage Lab); Daisy Ames,
Bernadette Baird-Zars, Adam Frampton,
Ericka Mina Song, Erin Purcell, and
Juan Sebastian Moreno (The Housing
Lab, Columbia University Graduate
School of Architecture, Planning and
Preservation); Sérgio Burgi, Farès
el-Dahdah, Alida C. Metcalf, and
David Heyman; Laura Fregolent and
Paola Malanotte-Rizzoli; Sandra Frem
and Boulos Douaihy; Sourav Kumar
Biswas and Rahul Mehrotra;
MIT Media Lab City Science group;
Bekim Ramku; Daniel Talesnik;
Sampson Wong and Merve Bedir

Managing Editor
Ala Tannir

Copy Editor
Rachel Valinsky

Editorial Assistance
Kathleen Pongrace

Design
Omnivore, Inc.

La Biennale di Venezia
Editorial Activities and Web

Head
Flavia Fossa Margutti

Editorial Coordination
Maddalena Pietragnoli

© La Biennale di Venezia 2021

All Rights Reserved under international
copyright conventions. No part of this
book may be reproduced or utilised in
any form or by any means, electronic or
mechanical, including photocopying,
recording or any information storage and
retrieval system, without permission in
writing from the publisher.

Printed on Munken Lynx made
out of cellulose from forests and
supply chains run with respect
for the environment, and socially
and economically sustainable

For Italian Distribution
ISBN 9788898727544

For International Distribution
by Silvana Editoriale
ISBN 9788836648603

La Biennale di Venezia
First Edition May 2021

Cover:
Image collage by Omnivore, Inc. using
adapted photographs by Shaun Anyi,
Wissam Chaaya, flowcomm,
G. Marcoaldi, Ciro Miguel, MIT Future
Heritage Lab, MIT Media Lab City
Science group, Robert Polidori /
Instituto Moreira Salles, Ibai Rigby,
and Tsang Tsz Yeung

Printed by Grafiche Antiga